AMERICAN High School Poets
Fall 2023

Live Poet's Society of NJ

edited by Dwight Edward Dieter

Copyright ©2023 by the Live Poet's Society of NJ as a compilation.

ISBN # 9798860433359

Copyrights to individual poems remain the property of the authors themselves. The poems contained within this Anthology were submitted to the Publisher by the authors noted. Such authors have certified them to be their own original work. Based upon such certification, and to the best of the Publisher's knowledge, all poems were written by the authors listed. The Live Poets Society of NJ bears no responsibility for misrepresented work, and any such responsibility shall be borne by those who claim to be copyright holders.

All rights reserved under International and Pan-American copyright conventions. No part of this book may be reproduced, stored in a retrieval system or transmitted in any form without written permission of the publisher and the individual copyright owners involved. Address all inquiries to the
Live Poets Society of NJ,
P.O. Box 8841,
Turnersville, NJ, 08012

Of Faith and Inspiration

To Death

Harken, Hades, to my words
And listen to my cry.
Harken, Sheol, I will speak
Once more before I die.

In malice, you have sought to claim
My dying for your own,
To make my eyes despair in you
And turn my heart to stone.

I was little more than dead –
A soul within a corpse –
But now, O Hell, I have found hope
A living, breathing, source.

A hope that lives in a living God
Whom death could not restrain.
He breathed out life so life could live
And made me for His name.

If He has given up His life
To claim me as His own,
Then you, O Death, have lost your hold,
For I am His alone.
Titus Webster, NH, Homeschooled

The Light

Lights were dim
There was no way I could win
My eyes were open, but I couldn't see
Everything was spinning around me
Mind was lying, couldn't even be a friend to me
But there you were waiting
The
Whole
Time
To my rescue, you delivered me
From every captivating thought and thing
that bound me
Now I am no longer blind
For you, my true friend
Are the way, the truth, and the life!
The light illuminating in my life
Thank you for saving me,
Jesus Christ
Avi Hill, OK, Ardmore High School

2- Of Faith and Inspiration

A Heart's Thoughts

In twilight's embrace, where dreams unfold,
A tapestry of words, a story yet untold.
Across the vast expanse of verse and rhyme,
A poem dances, a fleeting moment in time.

Like whispers of wind on a summer's eve,
Each line weaves a tale, with beauty to conceive.
Through realms of imagination, it takes flight,
Guiding hearts on a journey, both day and night.

The sunlit meadows, where wildflowers sway,
Painted with hues of gold in nature's grand display.
The gentle rain, a symphony on rooftops played,
Cleansing the earth as melodies are conveyed.

Through lofty mountains, their peaks kiss the sky,
And rivers that flow, their secrets never shy.
The moon's soft glow, casting a silvery glow,
Illuminating dreams that only poets know.

Love's tender touch, a soft caress in the air,
Igniting flames of passion, an eternal affair.
Heartaches and triumphs, in verses they reside,
Binding souls together, hearts no longer hide.
Charisma Carter, TX, Waltrip High School

Wonders of the Seasons

The Autumn trees once colored
Tinted with glee

The frosty breath of winter
Blows through the woodlands
Corrupting the joyful trees

Leaving dreary lands
Leaves dead and decayed
Trees barren of joy
Of hollow hearts

Spring breezes filled with wonder
Forests bloom with verdant gold
Emeralds under the sun
Glistening with delight
Gryffin Daniel Wallwork, NC, Northern Guildford HS

Of Faith and Inspiration - 3

Murrah Building Bombing

In twilight's hush, a whispered tale,
Of love's embrace, a fragile sail.
A symphony played by gentle breeze,
Caressing fields and ancient trees.

Golden hues adorn the sky,
As day bids the sun goodbye.
Stars emerge, twinkling bright,
Guiding us through the velvet night.

Whispering leaves, a rustling sound,
Nature's chorus all around.
Moon's soft glow, a silver thread,
Weaving dreams as we lay in bed.

Time's fleeting dance, swift and fast,
Each heartbeat a treasure, meant to last.
Embracing life's beauty, both big and small,
Grateful for the gifts, we cherish them all.

In this fleeting journey we embark,
Let kindness be our eternal mark.
For in these lines, a truth we find,
Love's the poetry of humankind.
Iliana Ashford, OK, El Reno High School

Healing the Scars of Asian Hate

In shadows cast by ignorance and spite,
A poison spreads, dividing hearts in pain,
Asian souls endure the endless night,
As hate's cruel flames engulf, leaving a stain.

From distant lands, a rich tapestry weaves,
A culture's beauty, stories to unfold,
Yet bias blinds, and empathy deceives,
Till hearts are cold, compassion's fire controlled.

But let us rise against this tide of hate,
Unite as one, with hands and hearts entwined,
For in diversity, we find strength's gate,
To heal the wounds and prejudice unbind.

In unity, we conquer darkness' might,
With love and understanding as our light.
Leilah Hilliker, AZ, Apollo High School

Before the Dawn

How sooner will the sunset come?
Oh quickly end the day
Before my heart held now ajar
Could shut its door and fade

How ever often will it break?
How weary I have been
If end days tears came hastily
And I shut out to Him

"Wake fast, oh soul, and lift your eyes
Do not pretend to pray
Your wicked heart's deceitfulness
Could draw your eyes away

Look up right here and breath in deep
Don't turn your heart to stone
The only thing I ask of you
Is look to Me alone

Before the dawn shall wear you down
I will not leave you lone
Stay strong, my child, and bear your part
I'll lead you safely home"
Alyssa Willett, NH, homeschooled

The Question of What

A dog may bark
A parrot might be smart
A cat can purr
A ghost may murmur
The question of ability
And perhaps utility
Is what can I do?
I cannot bark
I do not always feel smart
I do not purr
And I rarely murmur
Though I have doubts
I will not pout
I will continue to carry on
Until the last drop dawn
Though resolve may not seem like much
To me it feels like God's touch
Alexa Muirhead, KY, Muirhead's Homeschool

Of Faith and Inspiration - 5

Midnight

Dark and beauty come to mind
As I stare into your abyss
Seeing strange comfort
As cold air touches my skin
As though a mother caresses a child

Even so the shadows hidden in you
Give fright and cause panic
The only light to which withers them away
Is the only light in the midnight, the borrowed light
This light, this borrowed light,
Provides comfort like a father
Protecting a child

Together, provide the comfort and care of a lover.

As a child the memories of the same did not feel the same
As they were much bigger and scarier
But as we grow similar to the rise of that borrowed light
We realizes its a beacon to which represent the comforts
Of a new day
And we realize its not big nor it an enemy
But rather a guiding hope that we will move to that new day.
Julianna Taylor, FL, Palm Beach Gardens Community High School

Today

If today was yesterday,
What changes would you make?
The futures bright, and looming large,
You could fix every mistake

But if today is yesterday,
Then tomorrow if today
So take this moment as a special gift
And never look away

The problems we see so clearly now
How could we ever predict
So look today on towards tomorrow
Find the evil we must restrict

The future is a scary thing,
But it's truly here to stay,
So if we want a better future,
The future starts today.
Brendan Rubel, MA, Arlington High School

6- Of Faith and Inspiration

The Means to Pray

Sweaty palms tremble, clasp tightly together.
In between, a thin stick made of bamboo.
Aromas of
Forgiveness,
Freedom,
And purpose waft through the hazy air.
My throat feels thick with frankincense, voice suppressed.
My heavy feet shuffle up sacred stairs of stone,
A path seems to have already been made for me,
I look up.
I hear a harmony of prayers sung, sent to the gods
Who come from above the sky, under the sea,

And I come from a song of given opportunity,
From immigrant parents,
And of long lost dreams.

A deity made of gold, wisdom, intimidation, stands before me.
I give a pleading look to my mom, unsure of what to do,
But her soul, mind, and body face towards her savior with synergy;
Mirroring her whole, with my eyes shut,
I pray.
Emily Chao, CA, Northgate High School

Seeds for a Time without Flowers

When the clock will no longer tick
Who will hear what I have to say?
Is what I've done enough to stick?
Now there are no flowers left for a bouquet

Will my work have any use
Or was it all in vain?
Because now there is no forest and no spruce
And nobody left to feel any pain

When the Earth stops it great trek
Through the endless stars and sky
Will there even be a speck
To which my name I can apply?

My work may not be known
Millions of years from now
But the seeds that may be sown
Shall be planted anyhow
Isaac Sanders, GA, Strong Rock Christian School

Of Faith and Inspiration - 7

She was

She went to school, just like everyone else.
She struggled and studied, just like everyone else.
She dressed up, just like everyone else.
She dressed down, just like everyone else.
She was a person, just like everyone else;
but she was never allowed to be
just like everyone else.

No one else was ostracized from their entire community.
No one else was banned from performing and playing.
No one else was told they should hate themselves.
No one else was told they should kill themselves.
No one else was punished for just existing;
no one else
was transgender.

She was a woman, but was buried as a man.
She should have had more time, but she was buried in her youth.
No one cared that everyone killed her.

She was alive.
Hate kills
Nikolai Thaman, OH, Hilliard Bradley High School

Butterfly Insanity

The egg has hatched
A new life formed
The caterpillar has been born
The unique trio of colors on its back
Helping it move

The chrysalis has appeared
A new life formed
Its strings wrapped around its body
In a perfect circular motion
Helping it hold onto a branch

The cocoon has broken
A new life formed
The butterfly emerges
And breaks free out of its shell
The bursts of the beautiful orange and black wings
Helping it fly away
To another new life being formed
Sharndeep Kaur, CA, Clovis East High

8- Of Faith and Inspiration

The Greatest Mystery

Life is given to us
Don't take it for granted
The tick tock sound of a clock of life
Ringing in my ears reminding me of the end
There are struggles, it's normal
There are positives go search for them
Life is short, but it takes time
Like a new film of the century coming out in theaters
Don't wait for a purpose, make yourself known
Be that kind of person you never had
The darkness calls your name through the worst of times
Your mind like a deadly love
Beautiful and yet so harmful at times
The light will conquer the dark bit by bit
No matter how much life pushes you to your edge
You fight, you are good enough
The hatred intoxicating your mind
Like a best friend who just stabbed you in the back
There are people worth fighting for
Just go out there, search for those open doors
Yadira Ramos, TX, I.M. Terrell for STEM and VPA

Unveiling Society's Mask

Society wears a mask of perfection,
But beneath the surface, there's deception.
We're taught to hide our flaws and pain,
And to strive for wealth and fame.

We're told to fit into a mold,
To conform and never grow old.
To be like everyone else,
And silence our unique self.

But true beauty lies in imperfection,
In the raw and real expression.
Only when we're true to ourselves,
Can we find true happiness and wealth?

So let's break free from society's chains,
And let our true selves come to reign.
For only then can we truly see,
The beauty in humanity.
Tova Barenholtz, MD, Charles E Smith HS

Dear Universe

I understand the rules, and you did a great job.
On the sun, the grass, and especially
The long stretches of water that cannot be
Fathomed-- and everything inside.

I'm sorry, Universe, that it took me many years,
I'm sorry for being angry at the overbearing sun,
Or the grass for itching my skin,
Or my racing heart at the extremities of water.

I promise I was not trying to be bitter,
But I am human and you are cosmic,
And I could not understand the unwritten rules of living
To experience all that is beauty and love.

I really look up to you, Universe, literally, but also
For keeping the world motivated to keep spinning,
And letting things remain constant (as the sun rises)
Despite what we create, all that is unpredictable.
I understand the rules, and you did a great job.
Mindy Mailhot, GA, White County High School

Searching

How long until I find you?
Will it ever get easier,
or will it always be this hard?
I feel like I am chasing
after something that's not real.
And even if you are real
I am nothing you'd want,
stained and broken;
there is nothing you can do
to pick up the pieces.

I have always been here,
waiting for you.
You never needed to look for me.
You only needed to believe in me.
You have never needed to chase me,
for I have never left you.
And I never will.
Because you are something
I want to make new.
Marisol Walker, OK, Wesleyan Christian School

How We Are Forced To Think

We live in a hateful world
People can not say anything without being attacked
Without being hated for an opinion
We are a diverse world, so we think in different ways
Those around us believe what they think is the right way
That if you do not think like them you are automatically wrong
Why can't people have an open mind
Why can't people be right in their own opinion
Not according to others
Why must we live in a world that is determined by others
Why must we fear what we think
Why do we have to change who we are to please those around us
What if we were who we wanted to be
Without a thought of what others think
What if everyone had an open mind, and saw everything from every side
Maybe our world would be a little less hateful, filled with a little more love
Emma Melton, AL, Daphne High School

        Heaven's Gate

    The gentle, dropping, dripping rain
    Falls beneath a charcoal sky;
    Staring out, all see the pane,
    The deep darkness that draws one nigh.

    Lo! a light parts the clouds!
    The cold rain cedes itself to the blue dome,
    The sun shepherding away grave shrouds,
    But ushering in clouds of white foam.

    The breeze calms the gale;
    The birds soar through the air,
    Swiftly swooping as they sail
    On gusts sweeping this day so fair.
    Michael McGiffin, VA, The Heights School

        The Potter

    From the hands of the potter
    He molds
    He shapes
    He breaks
    He rebuilds
    He makes a masterpiece
    As chaos keeps spinning
    He makes a masterpiece
    He makes something extravagant
    From the hands of the potter
Judah Moye, TX, Lewisville High School

Of Faith and Inspiration - 11

The Struggle for Survival

The bombardment of rain berates the land.
My heavy soul with strong desire and passion.
Cannot bear but falter through life's demands.
When can I satisfy my hunger for satisfaction?
Cold piercing drops of water race down my skin.
My body aches with the stinging pains of fractures
I do so in hopes of being cleansed within.
Forever longing for even a moment of rapture.
As the frigid wind howls, it throws me aside.
My body fights, only to barely survive.
A maelstrom of my thoughts begin to collide.
Should I surrender or fight to survive?
Continuous attacks assault me, even as I reach the end.
I feel a sudden warmth around me, as my soul starts to ascend.
Jhaylin Cruz, MP, Marianas High School (Saipan)

Ode to the Thieving Gardener

With hands older than the earth that grew you
she will lift your rotten-apple body off the ground,
your limbs as limp as an overwatered cactus,
and carry you from the graveyard in which you were left.

And with arms sloshing, full of your water-wrinkled self
she must leave your friends behind as they count their worms
and plant you anew.
Jane A. Schmidt, CO, Grandview High School

Reign of Sun

Oh blue, hoary blue, timeless blue
Blue, who dominates the view
Of rippling waters, of rising sun
Of boats set out when the day's just begun
Oh blue, calm blue, familiar blue
Seen every day by all, who is nothing new
Who extends beyond the land in every which way,
leading ships of all sorts far beyond the grey
Oh rising sun, red sun, salient sun
Coloring droplets of water, one by one
Who, mixed with blue, molds a purple haze,
painting the horizon to start all days
Oh sun, nascent sun, peremptory sun,
Who comes when it wants, and listens to none
Who leaves its mark--its impression--on each,
swells of ocean in a port, grains of sand on a beach
Millena Taffere, TX, Cypress Ranch High School

12- Of Faith and Inspiration

Rosa

Her gnarled hands, the same motion
Undisturbed by the commotion,
The crowds and noises fade away
As kneeling in first light of day,
With quiet heart she bows her head,
Giving thanks for daily bread.
Forehead, chest, shoulder, shoulder,
Though she herself has become older,
The words she whispers ever fresh
As breathing in she draws His breath
The silence round her deepens till
The very sound of breath is still,
And in the quiet her heart syncs
To the rhythm of His beats
The worldly cares begin to cease
Daughter Father perfect peace

Maggie Phillips, TN, homeschooled

Grandmother

Once a wise woman told me,
To go and live out life,
To pursue every dream,
And accomplish every fight.
To live life to its fullest,
And slowly worry about stress,
To take life slowly,
Using each and every breath.
Using the kind actions,
And the right kind of heart,
You can accomplish every dream,
All you have to do is start.

Hailey Desmarais, MA, Apponequet Regional High School

To Be Free

I am freedom. I am weightless. I am a
cool exhale. I am relief. And I am the equivalent
feelings of floating, flying, and rising. I am the most desired.
But with the loud thunder, the weight of the downpour, and
strikes of lightning, I can not be acquired. So do me a
favor in this stormy world and hold an umbrella for one whose wings
have curled. They will hold one for you. Soon the world will be
released from constant thunder- storms that make the wings
deform. Soon the world will swoon at the sight of the
differently colored wings that fly to the moon.
Wings of flight Wings of freedom

Fatima Diallo, RI, Cumberland High School

Of Faith and Inspiration - 13

Nature

Nature.
All but we start life in her presence
All but we finish life in her presence
All but we appreciate her
All but we see her beauty
All but we wish to connect
All but we wish to live with balance
Where we are all connected
Whether a stranger or partner
Everything is connected
To see her for what she is
Only innocent eyes may see her true beauty
Only those who truly want to see the connection may
Only those with pure intent
Only those who appreciate her any time
Only those who do not take her for granted.
Jadzia Williams, NC, Franklinton High

Plans

The Institution of my ideas, I call it a plan
A conclusion of something I truly understand
Then comes confusion as it slides into play
An illusion of night blocking out the day
With all my might I'll strip the shadow away
To see the light again, to see the new day
but to my great fright, my efforts gone stale
all that work to no avail, all that work just to fail
then the might of the light pierces a veil of the night
The illusion and confusion brought to their knees
a freezing of my fright, and a clarity in my sight
for an institution of ideas is forming quite near
ending this story for the conclusion is here
Joshua Palik, TN, Aliyah Academy

Celestial Adventure

On wings of destiny, I shall ascend,
Exploring the galaxies without end.
Dreams take flight in stellar array,
Discovering wonders both far and away.

I'll twirl with comets, race across the sky,
Journey through distant stars eclipsing my sight.
A celestial quest of unknown desire,
Venturing boldly into the infinite fire.
Jessica Meikle, NY, Queens High School of Teaching

14- Of Faith and Inspiration

Whispers of the Night

Through cracks of despair, light finds its way,
In the darkest of nights, it leads to the day.
Scars tell a story of strength and of grace,
Resilience blooms in the hardest of space.

The echo of laughter, a balm for the soul,
Mending what's broken, making us whole.
In the eyes of a stranger, connection is found,
Humanity's threads interwoven, unbound.

Time's flowing river, it carries our dreams,
Moments like ripples on infinite streams.
Seeking the answers, we journey within,
Unraveling truths in the silence therein.

Cherish each heartbeat, for life is a song,
A symphony of moments, both short and long.
Embrace the unknown, let your spirit take flight,
For in the depths of your being, lies endless light.

Taleen Hamed, FL, Saint Joseph School(Ramallah, Palestine)

The Storm

Dark, gloomy, and gray, the envelopment
Of the heart surrounded by the dark storm;
Devastation, and the thief of all joy,
The onslaught of misery, wave by wave,
Menacing clouds of war blot out the sun,
Torrents falling upon the suffering soul;
Tears throughout the night; in the morning, pain

Through this trial speak to me, O Father;
Teach me Your ways, so far above my own.
You are both sovereign and good, this I know.
Comfort me within this grief and sorrow
Bring joy to me when it has disappeared
And yet when all hope has abandoned me
You'll be my peace in the heart of the storm

Ellie Andersen, AZ, Veritas Academy of Tucson

Flawless Shape

An awesome figure
Mirrored sides
Equal and balanced
Identical at every angle
Solid and defined
No faults detected
Absolutely perfect
To be a square...

Tiana Roundtree, SC, Cane Bay High School

Of Faith and Inspiration - 15

Past, Present, and Future

Deep in every one of us is a yearning to change and grow
To leave behind the evils that once hid and trapped our souls
At times while we are shedding that filthy layer of skin
We get lost and downtrodden, focused only on where we've been

We halt our forward motion with sight that's solely retrospective
We miss the present and it's joys which we haven't yet detected
Daily opportunities and blessings change our lives
But if we overlook them, we will never really thrive

The future could be anything, we get to make it happen
We can be someone new, do whatever we imagine
We can look towards the future anticipating peace
We can make it happen, and our fulfillment will increase

The past prompts contemplation
The present is for participation
The future offers motivation
Fate is determined by imagination
Samantha Cammack, UT, Bonneville High School

Life in Seasons

I don't have control over my own emotions.
The weather does.
Summer is where I'm at my all time high,
Enjoying ice cream on the boardwalk,
Smelling the salty waves of the mighty ocean,
All in the 95 degree weather accompanied by the sun.
But now it's fall.
The leaves crinkle as I stomp on them,
Out of frustration and longing for summer.
The weather is abnormally cold,
Just like my new persona
In this season.
But the trees take on a new identity,
Sparking my realization
That just like how the seasons change,
My life is changing for the better too.
Emily Vu, PA, Marple Newtown High School

Prince of Peace

Afraid to pray
Afraid to fall
I wonder if He's there at all
Do crying babes feel someone's arms
That cradle them, protect from harm?
Or do they weep with blind belief
That faithful shepherds steadfast keep
That angels that they've never seen
Will guard the beauty of their dreams?
That mothers will always be there
To kiss their cheeks and brush their hair?
The faith I cannot seem to keep
As war and famine shake the streets
As history replays, repeats
As shards of glass stick through our feet
Is faith a baby knows so deep
The faith that guards a soldier's sleep
And faith like that, i have to say
Makes life's worst heartaches worth the pain.
Reese Weicht, FL, Newsome High School

A Tribute To All

For all that we could give,
And the effort we exhume,
There would be no greater reward,
Than for me to learn from you.
And little do you know,
The impact that you make,
Comes through neither fame nor gain of wealth,
But through the values, seeds you've sown,
And presence that you emanate.
But do not think the things you do
Go without notice,
For though no one may seem to care
This is only for the moment.
Your face will be forgotten,
Your name a lost word,
But what you left behind to be,
Will never fade throughout,
The pages of our history.
Emily Marin, TX, Homeschooled (Abeka Homeschool)

Of Faith and Inspiration - 17

Play

You are an instrument. So play.
Let your notes buzz harshly like erratic
bumble bees before softening into a butterfly's wave.
Create a story with your tune,
weaving melodic silk threads into a colorful tapestry for all to gaze upon.
Control the pitch, rhythm, and speed independently,
distinct in how well they melt into each other.
Gather everyone in close to listen at first,
and once you've built a crowd,
flourish the feeling in your song.
Let elation wash them over, sorrow ache in their cores, rage rattle through their streets.
Most importantly, enjoy yourself.
Cradle your spirit high above the summit of your
disappointments where all can hear it echo best.
Collectively, we are a symphony.
Play.
Asha Richardson, OH, Columbus Alternative High School

Beating Back the Forest

These trees I did not plant and yet they flourish.
If I cannot beat them back, I must succumb.
No matter how I fight they find their nourish.
They grow with gusto, attitude and gum.

They mock me as I merely mask progression.
All I do is futile in their face.
One respite I can hope for is regression.
Then they return and stand fast in their place.

So why do I defend my plot with vigor?
And why should I so futilely proceed
to fight with no success the raging succor,
when they so desperately my garden need?

These vines are not the vines of hope and vision.
They are the vines of negligence and void.
Wantonly they grow as weeds, not wisdom.
To beat them back is momentary joy.

As years go by my field becomes a forest.
Death taunts me as I trim his seeds of sin.
The struggle which has raged on here before us
is one the Devil's won so deep within.

Yet, still I say, "Fear not this futile mission.
For when our lives we feel have no avail,
our God can force all evil to submission
and in the end the righteous will prevail."
Dwight E Dieter, NJ, editor

18- Of Faith and Inspiration

*Of Love
and
Dedication*

Protagonists

I remember the way I stared at you,

"Don't stare at the sun, it's too bright for your eyes. It'll hurt you."
But you were brighter than the sun, brighter than any star in this galaxy,
And I stared at you for so long.

You once told me it's not impossible.
My whirlwind of doubt, I thought would extinguish you.
But you only burned brighter and my worry melted.
Not impossible, just hard.

Nature does not woo me, and I do not fall at the feet of the sky,
But what a joy to indulge in your majesty. Gold floods my senses;
My grief has found a boundary.

Say goodbye to the weariness, to the sorrow and lament and melancholy.
My soul weeps in your presence, such a feeling would be a sin to replicate.

Unfathomable glory, I could cheer you on for eternity.
Watching you soar higher every day, as I wipe the stardust from my cheeks,
This ringing in my ears screams for devotion.

How many times must I stare until I wither away?
Are our paths eternally intertwined?
All this time later, you still capture my attention — my devotion.

And you stare back.

Azure Klusek, MI, Skyline High School (Ann Arbor)

Sleepless Nights Thinking About You

Every morning, every night, you and I
Stare at each other, earnestly longing.
Though our moments are short and rare, I try
To indulge in your sense of belonging.

When I am without you, my world turns gray.
My eyes droop, no longer in the daylight
That I escape from with each coming day—
Piercing my thoughts with agonizing plight.

I need you, your warmth, your compelling gaze.
As your gentle cuddles of fervent bliss
Always leave me running back to your space.
You're the only one I await to kiss.

Goodnight. As you tuck me in bed, I weep:
"I'm so tired, I love you, my dear sleep."
Diana Akhmedova, NY, Stuyvesant High School

20 –Of Love and Dedication

Words left unsaid

All of the words left unsaid might make the difference between life and death

Disbelief at the words *died by suicide*
I wait for the punchline to hit,
For the room to burst into laughter
As you walk through the door
Unscathed and grinning

Dark blue is how I feel at the thought of your struggles,
The emotions you masked
With a joke and the biggest smile
Which could elicit a happiness
From others that you hated yourself
for knowing you would never feel

Today I saw your chair sitting empty
And couldn't help but wonder when you would arrive
Bag slung over one shoulder, scuffed sneakers
Signaling the commencement of class
And easing the anxious expressions on tear stained cheeks

How to save lives was the title of today's lesson,
But it's too late

No time could lessen the pain

Lyla Pak, CA, Polytechnic High School

        drizzle

        rain kisses
        the concrete.
        i press my
        eyes to the glass,
        wishing i
        could absorb
        the water
        the clouds
        the way your hand
        feels in mine.
        i miss your
        rainwater eyes,
        your raven hair.
        the clouds collide,
        murmuring,
        the sound reminiscent
        of your quiet voice.

Danielle Doran, TN, Homeschool

Admiration

I stop to see your garden,
It is vivid and complex.
I hear familiar buzzing,
So I follow with swift steps.

Standing by the path beside
Are yellow crape myrtle trees.
And hanging from the largest branch—
A hive of honeybees.

Frothy, fertile florets,
Yielding fragrances sublime.
I wander and become absorbed,
Oblivious to the passing of time.

And if I seek perfection
I will never be content.
Although, your garden grows so marvelously—
It must be heaven-sent.

And at some point I wander away,
Trailing leaves behind.
So you won't know that I have been here,
Inside your golden mind.
Victoria Hoeper, MN, Osakis High School

Painting

My mother is a paint brush
Always, she bends, unwaveringly
Her body making rainbows, never
Ceasing
She sits, another stroke
Palms pressed, another stroke
The colors blur as she murmurs the Holy Dialogue
Spit splashes on the canvas
Her eyes take a long, deep bow
But how is it that even the ancient moon quivers in their brightness
Tubes of paint pop open
Her lips fasten
Her strokes deepen
Rainbows slicing through the air
Her hair drawing curtains, dimming lights
Within her heart and soul, the bristles quietly ignite
Smoke floats like clouds all around, even when
Pff! The spark goes out and
Nothing, and everything, remains
Kellye Nguyen, CA, Brewster Academy

Whispers of the Aching Heart

In depths of sorrow or joy's embrace,
A heart's ache finds its dwelling place.
It swells within, a bittersweet tide,
Emotion's rush, impossible to hide.

When sadness grips, a heavy weight,
Each beat echoes with a mournful fate.
Tears cascade, a torrential rain,
Melancholy's melody, a haunting refrain.

Yet, in moments of bliss, the ache remains,
Love's tendrils weaving through tender veins.
A symphony of happiness, sweet and pure,
A heart's ache, a sensation to endure.

For within the pain, a truth unfolds,
A testament to life's stories untold.
It reminds us we're alive, fiercely so,
In every ebb and flow, highs and lows.

So let the ache reside, a constant hum,
A reminder that our souls are one.
For in the depths of our heart's embrace,
The ache reveals life's intricate grace.
Lucy Hernandez, CA, Bellflower High School

Letter to A. Gong

Dear A. Gong,
They lured you away with the promise of chickens
Chickens to raise and feed your growing family
They took you
Was it because you were a successful businessman from the city?
Or was it because your grandparents were from China?
Did you know what was coming?
Did you know you would never get to see your children grow?
Did you know you would never grow old?
To be immortalized in a portrait
Forever young
Forever smiling
A small smile, full of secrets from the past
Such a large family, united then, scattered now
Everyone remembers you, but they don't talk about you
You left with the soldiers and never came back
Everyone assumes you were killed
You are probably buried in the middle of nowhere
6ft under in a mass grave, never to be seen again.
Melissa Yos, CO, William Smith High School

Of Love and Dedication - 23

Seven Hundred and Thirty Days

As we sit in the parking lot
Drinking watered down lemonade from our red solo cups
And laughing about the night we just had
My mind drifts back to the many other nights we've since lost

It's been two years since I last saw you
Though it felt much longer than just seven hundred and thirty days
Your hair has grown out, and the curls inherited from your mom finally coil
You've gotten your ears pierced, which I know your dad probably loathes

You tell me stories from the past two years
Who you've dated, who you've grown out of
I tell you my tales too, which seem dull compared to yours
And yet you smile through each one

So much between us has changed
Neither of us are the same person we used to be
But here we sit, in my same car from high school
Rambling on about both nothing and everything all at once

You stare at me
And I steal a glance at you
Both two years older
But still as hopelessly in love as before
Kacie Sproul, TX, Brandeis High School

To Jirón

In shadows cast by love's sweet glow,
I found a partner, heart aglow.
Hand in hand, we faced life's dance,
A tender bond, a true romance.

Yet time, unkind, did intervene,
Tearing dreams like a ruthless machine.
Gone is the touch that once I knew,
In solitude, I now pursue.

The echoes of laughter, they still ring,
Memories dance, but bittersweet sting.
A void resides where once love thrived,
In the realm of memories, we are forever tied.

But though the pain may never subside,
I will carry the love once personified.
For in the depths of my heart, you will stay
Forever cherished, come what may.
Adanahi Hernandez, PA, Norristown Area High School

24 –Of Love and Dedication

Eternal Loves Journey

In dreams, a boy's heart sought release,
In dreams, his longing found sweet peace.
Through his grandma's love, anguish would cease,
Through her love, his soul found sweet release.

They danced through days, wild and free,
Exploring life's wonders, joyful and free.
But fate dealt a blow, cancer's cruel might,
Shadows cast, dimming their light.

In final moments, hands clasped with grace,
Whispers of love, tears streaking his face.
Her spirit soared, from earthly tether,
Leaving memories to cherish forever.

To the boy, healing from heart's sear,
Memories guide, calming the fear.
Hold onto love, let the tears cascade,
In sadness, her spirit won't fade.

In enduring love, strength will ensue,
In enduring love, resilience will pursue.
Her spirit forever shines through,
Her spirit forever embraced, renewed.
Preston Aguila-Velez, GA, Allatoona High School

Waves

your love is like the sea
and I'm the shore
still
every now and then you rush towards me
your waves completely engulfing me
and i'm indulged in that feeling once again
comfort
warmth

but it only lasts for a moment
for then you are pulled back
by something

or someone

leaving me in disarray
and I can't do anything but wait
wait for you to wash all over me again
and again
Legend Kuate, TX, La Marque HS

Of Love and Dedication - 25

Silent Flames: Love in Shadows

In shadows we find solace, hearts entwined,
A secret love, hidden from the world's design.
Closeted souls, fearing what may come,
Yet loving each other, we find freedom.

We deny, we hide, our loves held inside,
While others suspect, we silently confide.
Acting "straight" for all to see,
Though our hearts beat true, longing to be free.

Parents trying to set us up, blind to the truth,
But our hearts are bound, unyielding, uncouth.
In stolen moments, our love takes flight,
A refuge from the world's prying sight.

In this hidden love, we take our stand,
Defying expectations, holding hand in hand.
Though in shadows we dwell, our love is real,
A flame burning strong, a secret we conceal.

In whispering promises, we find our grace,
Yearning for a love that society can't trace.
We'll cherish each other, our soul alight,
For in this secret love, our hearts ignite.
Jeffrey Chen, NJ, McNair Academic High School

Dear Rosebud

Draw close, Rosebud,
Come here and hither,
It pains me, rosebud,
Your petals wither,

And one by one and fold and drop.
As so many tears are a part of a soul,
So your rose petals are part of you,
Dear Rosebud.

Had I the power to hold petals together,
Or had I the power to cease sorrow's death,
But nay, I have but power to hold you,
Dear Rosebud.

Quiet now, Rosebud. Reserve your strength.
Fewer petals is not less beautiful.
Quiet now, Rosebud. Rest in peace.
You must wither away in the morrow.
Declan Quinn Gibson, FL, Homeschooled

Pinky Promise

Our fingers intertwined in a vow made blind
Pledging to open a daycare together to raise a family together
to exist together to breathe together
A promise that would weigh nothing on your conscious
Filled with the void of only your darkness

Our souls intertwined schedules realigned
To sacrifice sleep and family and friends and work and sanity
For one more second one more smile one more sigh
one more giggle one more soft whisper one more
Nothing

Our hearts intertwined to love unconfined
Falling into anything into your open arms into your princess blanket
into your white leaf into your presence
My comfort my angel
How stupidly faithful

Our thoughts intertwined to think as one to laugh as one to sleep as one
to lay as one to sing as one to speak as one to live as one
I must have won
You? Breaking a pinky promise?
Never
Ria Mohan, WA, Juanita High School

Saffron

As I ponder, listening to the frogs, the wind squanders.
My ribs burrow at the consideration of you. I pine.
You've kissed the back of my legs. That no one has
done before–
Only the sun, and the mosquitoes swarming up my limbs reached that distance.
I'd slaughter to become the clothes that drape over your cold caramelized skin.
When we kiss you taste like sweet kool-aid, sparking at the wisp of my tongue,
I watch you, as you stare beyond my gaps and fixate on the appeal.
Craving the dirt beneath our feet, until we feel the grit in your teeth.
Dissect me. You can see the sprouts buried in my organs, the seeds,
that you have split, now becoming mature.
I long to be the blood pumping through your weakened gums,
To be the mush between your crooked teeth.
Grant me permission to sulk inside of you.
Let me germinate my melancholy throughout your nerves, and veins.
Through disease, I'm grasping onto you.
And at night,
I listen to the rats under my pillow and think of your heart-piercing through your chest.
What I desire: is to be at peace with lying down in your field of saffron, to dissolve.
My necessity? To be smothered by your praise, and to become inflicted with your presence.
Haley (Shiloh) Sizemore, KY, Cordia High School

Of Love and Dedication - 27

this is how it began and this is how it ends

all the strength manifested your flesh swollen
    holding a pen
grinding my skin into splinters off the cross
i'm going to choke
 if you
don't let go

        don't let go

i etched your memory into my skin
watch as it scabs over
suffer the burn
stretching the margin
so hard. so desperately
your skin shreds off the nails

bend over to stop me from
going over
reach across   to touch me
find yourself upside
            down
drown in the tears of love
watch as you scab over

Lyla Yango, AZ, Desert Mountain High School

Oh Mother, How Mother

Oh Mother, How mother can your love be so enchanting
Oh Mother, your love shines like a meteor burning through the night sky
Your love is an endless expanse where galaxies dance in an infinite embrace
An infinite embrace that holds no bounds or limits like the vast stars and dreams
Dreams that some see as only desires and wishes like the wishing star
You make me see dreams as a course with a few rocky asteroids that can be overcome
Through all the ups and downs, near or far, your love is the star in the sky leading me on

Oh Mother How Mother can you be so endearing
How Mother can your tender embrace make my heart flutter like a butterfly
Like the pollen it carries, your love carries with me everywhere I go
Through the dull and bleak storms that surround my presents in reality
You keep my wings from becoming heavy and damaged
You help my wings flourish and lead me to the sky where all is endless

Your love so enchanting and endearing with the pure glow of a halo-like ring
Like Mother Mary, your love is everlasting and enshrined in my heart since my first light
Since my first light, I could see and feel love even though I never knew the word
Oh Mother you help me grow my wings and lead me to a beautiful flower full of beauty
How Mother can your love be so endless, with a heart the size of your fist, that makes even the vast universe seem small

Thalia Fuentes, AZ, Arizona Agribusiness & Equine Center

28 –Of Love and Dedication

Between Held Hands

There's something so special about holding hands
It is easily the most beautiful act of love there is
I hold your hand as we cross the street
I hold your hand so I cannot lose you in a crowd
I hold your hand to tell you I'm sharing this moment with you
Your hands have the power of the World
Hands have built Pyramids from simple stone
Hands have mapped the land they discovered
Your hands are the result of the hands of those who have loved each other

Our hands are the gateway to life
The gateway to every possibility known to man
When humans are born, we navigate the world through our hands
By memorizing the touch of our loved ones
And by some force outside of the Universe
Our gateways to the World have found each other
Through our intertwined fingers
I hold all of your thoughts
Hold all of your fights
All of your love

I'll hold them as long as you allow it.

Gabriella Guerra, TX, Vista Ridge High School

The Color Blue

rain pouring out my window during long nights
tapping the glass like little steps
talking about how we could take flight
but only when it feels right

...blue reminds me of you

jumping in puddles
rain drops tend to cuddle
acting if we were kids once more
not knowing what's to come forth

...blue reminds me of you

wishing we had another hour
while not knowing you were the one
who stopped the timer
draining thoughts come and go
just as fast as you did

...blue sadly reminds me of you

Adelia Nasir, MI, Lake Shore HS & Macomb Mathematics and Science Technology Center

Of Love and Dedication

Magical Moonlit Waltz

and it was with this, the stars appeared
the sun had long since said
"goodnight"
and the moon had brought its young'uns out
to dance and play in his light.

and it was with this, a simple pair with matching souls
sprawled out to see this magical moonlit waltz
millions of souls in the sky finding their mate,
each with their own routine
dancing to the same tune around the same moon

and it was with this, the simple pair of matching souls
rose from their gazing to join the moon dance.
the tune was slow
the souls became one, swaying beneath the sky
surrounded by souls only alight in the night

and it was with this, all of these souls
single, or with their matching pairs
each with their own dance
were joined by the simple pair with matching souls
as they found their own groove in this stellar midnight promenade.
Charlotte Lovell, CT, Fairfield Warde High School

To Nonno, A Promise

In familiar spaces
I turn the corners,
hoping I'll find you there.
And, in your absence,
despite my brief dejection,
I am reminded not to despair.

For I need not look with my eyes,
but call upon my memories
and reach out with my heart,
to see you; standing there,
supporting my endeavors
and rooting for my success,
as I know you will forever.

And please, do not fret, Nonno.
For although you are gone now,
your legacy does not end here.
It will live on through those you held dear.
Your impact and your teachings
will carry on for eternity,
never to be forgotten.
Nate Bullinger, MO, Ladue Horton Watkins High School

30 –Of Love and Dedication

My Own

My art is mine and I can say that with pride.
For years I've been looking, searching for that thing to call mine
The blank wall on all sides provided that for me
The hole that I had to get out of
While in that hole I did what I was good at I wrote
I wrote until my hand cramped from holding the crayon slowly dying out
My art is mine
No one could take it away from me but myself
The crayon died out
But there I found five more
Each one getting their time to shine
One day the crayons will run out
Then what will be mine
The empty crayon box full of stubs
And the beautiful art sculpture I made
In blood my name
Jayden White, IL, Kenwood Academy High School

Garden of Sapphire

The Garden of Sapphire, an old tale.
Full of fascination, full of wonder
A place full of flowers, frail and divine
Sometimes it sprinkles, sometimes it thunders
There lay the blue boy, sleepy and torpid
Always dreamt about a fallen being
There he sat, staring at the blue orchid
Thinking about it, was he foreseeing?
The flowers then flowed and swayed in the wind
Something felt off, his heart started to race
Faster and faster it whirled, swirled, and spinned
Till he saw, then his heart was set in place
There she was, the girl he has always seen
The one and only, his red Ruby queen.
Angela Carandang, CA, Panorama High School

That of Icarus

By you, my blinding star,
I am bound to the same fate which plagued Icarus.
I am bound to soar too high,
and to fly far too close,
only to meet your eyes for a single moment.

From your blinding aura,
I watch as my wings have begun to melt;
and I see drops of melted wax and my tears consolidate.
As I fall, I see you slowly drift away,
out of my reach, whilst I haven't a single limb to grasp.
Jacob Staed, KY, Tates Creek High School

Of Love and Dedication - 31

Simple Devotion

Crooked teeth.
Crooked Hands.
Crooked Nose.
An imperfect reflection of my imperfect ancestors
And you love their latest installment.
I hope they know that you and
Me are as mundane as them
And them, and them.
I know I'm not religious anymore
But I see how you carefully pluck
Each seed from a pomegranate
Just to surprise me with a treat after work.
I know a saint when I see one.
You hand me the bowl and I'm
Blessed by the divine.

Valens Bandy, CA, Sage Creek High School

L.O.V.E.

Love, a tender flame that softly glows,
In hearts entwined, its beauty shows.
A whispered word, a gentle touch,
Love's magic, oh, it means so much.
A shared smile, a knowing glance,
Love's sweet embrace, a joyful dance.
Through ups and downs, it remains strong,
Love's melody, a timeless song.
In love's embrace, we find our peace,
A bond that brings our souls release.
Love's simple truth, forever true,
In every heartbeat, I love you.

Adyanna English, CO, Cherry Creek High School

all or none

My untouched mattress suddenly soiled
The edges are frayed, hems undone
A sunspot dimples the middle:
My personal melting pot
I normally sleep outside
The itchy grass lifting my body up
Where I traverse the lonely galaxy
But tonight, we'll rot together
Because aren't we made of stardust?
Like residual stains left in a pot
We'll burn together on this mattress
Because space is so vast, and we are burning so fast.

Lily Turcotte, MN, Pequot Lakes High School

32 –Of Love and Dedication

Break you beautifully

You want forever. I can't give you that, but I promise you this: Come with me and I will show you incredible things in ordinary places. Let me show you the reflection of the sunset on the lake, and the lives people carry on their shoes. I'll tell you how all your freckles connect like constellations and I'll trace them with my finger so you can see them too. I want to tell you beautiful stories about the pebble in your pocket and the trees outside your window. I can teach you magic: how to blow a dandelion just right, where the fairies live, moonlight kisses, and what love feels like. I will kiss you in every wondrous place and mend what others had broken. I will change you so much that you cannot help but see me everywhere. And when I leave, there will be nothing that does not taste like me, no song you have not heard me sing, no small detail I have not showed you, and no memory that does not have me in it. I will break you so beautifully that you will not wish to be mended and you will keep the ashes of our love on your shelf, immortalized forever more, for all to see.
Gabriella Smith, TX, ILTexas Aggieland High School

A2 Masterpiece

I arrived on a steamy, sticky, sweet summer day
You say you counted my fingers and toes,
Then kissed me on the nose.
You called me "perfect" even though I was wailing...wahhhh
I guess because I was your son
That our souls connected like swirls of paint blended to make a new color
We share so much; there is no doubt, everyone can see
From the date of our birth, our eyes, our hair,
Our A's and our love of art.
You have always painted a perfect world for me
Now the painting has changed in just a brush "stroke"
So I will do what is needed; I will take the brush like Van Gogh
To make sure our masterpiece is continued
It is the very least I can do.
Aiden Arrington, GA, Lassiter High School

When the Film Develops

Our faces are washed out by the bright flash of the Polaroid camera.
The paleness contrasts against the background of the school cafeteria,
making it appear pitch-black.
I'm not looking at the camera, and he neglected to smile.
A half-eaten lunch and empty milk carton find their way into the shot.
When the film develops,
I know it's a memory we will cherish forever.
Taken at the lunch table where we met,
Perfectly imperfect.
A Polaroid is forever.
Erika Gibson, TX, Lubbock-Cooper High School

Of Love and Dedication - 33

This Is What We Talk About When We Talk About Love

It is one lover calling to another,
two mouths eloping to meet each other in the middle of a bridge.
And if I'm no good?
I know.
Whole hours are being cut into minutes as we speak,
dollars into pocket change, grief into smaller grief.
I spend all my quarters to listen to you breathe on the other side.
Over the telephone, I am calling you. Mother & daughter,
a language notoriously hard to speak.

I am fourteen years old and lost in a grocery store.
Bit late to be doing that, you say.
Let me talk, I say. You shut up. This too is a form of love.
Outside my bedroom, the streetlight is a round moon, lending light
to the tiny flecked stars of rainwater that gather outside of my window.
Rainwater which has no light of its own, that lives only a day.
Because the night was dark and spooked, and it became impossible
to tell who was loved and who was loving.
If you could be a taker and a keeper, although nobody knows for sure.
If I could be the flame to your boiler,

the North to your South, and leave you enough either way.
You must know I sat, lonely with grief, that night. In the stillness, in the strain,
knowing pain was close, love maybe even closer.
Hannah Ahn, MD, Marriotts Ridge High School

The Lonely Bones Poem

There is beauty in bones.
Our lonely bones.
We're all just piles of
Bones. Lonely bones.
Aren't we all alike? Small, large, thin, thick, delicate, sturdy, curved
Piles of bones.
To me, your bones are beautiful.

And if I asked for my lonely bones to have a place beside yours...
Would you oblige?
What if I asked you if you'd still love me
If I was nothing but a small pile of bones? Would you... *Love me...*
Even if at the core, I'm just a pile of bones.
Would you listen?

I mean,
We've got our whole lives to figure it out. But beneath it all,
I want to know if my bones have found a resting place beside yours?

We're all just piles of bones
Trying to find a place to rest and a partner to hold.
Your lonely bones are beautiful to me.
Camryn Adams, HI, Punahou School

An Orange for our woes

Did you know the greeks used to eat oranges
because they believed it warmed their stomachs
That's why I stay with you
I believe behind the initial bitter taste you leave
Someday, a warmth may grow in my stomach
A warmth that triumphs the churning feeling you give me now
Since I have met you I have been so accustomed to nausea
Yet, I still I can't get away from you
Maybe you don't make me warm, but you make me feel
I have known you in many lives before my dear friend, in the last were not so cold
Did you know the greeks worshipped Ivy because they believed it symbolized eternal life?
Because no matter the conditions, Ivy always grows, even in the times it doesn't seem like to should be able to
I wish we could've grown together rather than apart
In another lifetime, we are two ancients greeks, sick to our stomach, orange in hand
In another lifetime were are warm.
Elizabeth Cornett, CA, South High School

Coconut

Coconut,
you hated it.
You didn't like its taste
nor its shavings,
or the smell.
The smell is what you hated most.
I remember that day all too well.
I did my hair with a bottle of Cantu,
you told me you could smell it even from
my clammy hands.
After that, I never used it
knowing how you felt.
You're gone now.
You've been gone for over a year
and yet I still haven't brought myself to finish off that bottle.
- I miss your smell
Autumn Moore, FL, Chain of Lakes Collegiate High School

He Notices

I've always loved the water
I've always called it my own
A few days ago, you said
"Water is your comfort zone"
And waves crashed inside my head
Because it's so deeply true
I've always loved the water
I think I've always loved you
Ava Thompson, WA, Homeschool

Of Love and Dedication - 35

Hunger

i am standing in my kitchen
it is 2am
there is nothing to eat

i went to the grocery store yesterday
i bought a pack of gum and a bar of soap
the fridge was full when i got home

i wonder:
is the fridge empty or is the kitchen?
what makes a fridge feel full?

there is only food to eat when there is love
sometimes i think i could eat my mother's love every day,
for the rest of my life

i still wouldn't be full

Chloe Charbonneau, TX, Rockwall High School

El Poder del Languaje (Power of Language)

In language's embrace, hearts entwine,
Unspoken words, a love design.
Each phrase, a brushstroke, paints the start,
Learning tongues, we share one heart.

Vowels sing in melodies so sweet,
Conjugated, love's heartbeat, complete.
Verbs, like rivers, swiftly flow,
In their currents, our passion grows.

Syntax weaves emotions, true and clear,
Grammar's art, love's atmosphere.
Adjectives bloom, vivid and bright,
Colors woven through the night.

In linguistic realms, together we roam,
In the language, we've found our home.
In words, we've built our love's grand chart,
Learning languages, you've captured my heart.
Casey Lawing, TX, Northwest Cabarrus High School

36 –Of Love and Dedication

A Letter from a Belt to a Four-Leaf Clover

    My leather can't compare to the simplicity of your nature.
I have holes in my body from heartbreaks that punctured my heart.
It's time for me to buckle down, and I want to buckle down with you.
    You are one in 10,000.
A rare beauty.
On a crowded field, you are the only one I see.
You may be similar to the others, but you are certainly not the same.
Love, faith, hope, and luck
are what remind me of you.
Love, faith, hope, and luck
are what I need to be mended from heartbreak.
    You are not as flexible as I am.
In fact, you are fragile.
So fragile that even the wind can break you.
But I will never hurt you, not now, and not ever.
    You may think I'm bizarre, but my love for you goes from head to hip.
I can only hope that your love gives me good luck,
and doesn't leave me with another hole in my leather.
I am rooted to you, and you are rooted to me.
Hasini Anireddy, NY, Guilderland High School

The Price of Love

Love is natural and freeing,
but all things must come at a price,
love is indefinite and amending in value.

The price of love is learning to disarm and disband the guards of your soul, the protectors of your heart,
you must open the locked door that leads to you,
to let someone see the healed and the damaged parts of you,
to love you must be willing, even if the cost is grave,
even if in the end, your guards are back at their posts & the door locks once more.

The price of love is making those exigently laborious choices.
the ones where you must choose to be silent or choose to be loud,
the ones where you must choose whether to yield or to challenge.

you must sacrifice for your love,
we all must sacrifice for our love,
we put our whole being on the line with the risk of destruction to ourselves.

And so, my love,
you have become my reason to rise but the cause of my downfall,
but in the end,
I regret none and will sacrifice it all, again and again,
but only for you.
Addison Scurek, FL, Venice Senior High School

Of Love and Dedication - 37

a casket of gold

am i the only one who senses,
a corpse in this bed,
we know we were a mistake,
even though it was never fake.
these things always die,
but we can bury the body.

you've already left it all behind,
leaving me to drag what we were,
over the black concrete,
under the beat red sky,
leaving some roots behind,
just incase it ever rains in hell.

the feeling of lifelessness,
meets an emotional collide,
love laced with dread,
thought to be a never ending high,
you always make me fold,
i leave us in a casket of gold.
Miles Benton, DE, Polytech High School

Where water meets land

Where water meets land,
Woman meets man.
The waves crash against the cliffs,
As love abounds in their midst's.

Deep blue water engulfs the coast
as his blue eyes boast a hope of love forever.
In the endeavor he sees the light casting through the quiet mist.
The storms at sea are no match for lovers however strong they may be.

The sea stands strong seldom caring of its wrongs.
Love and toils cast sorrow across the sunrise.
As the once strong lovers say goodbye.
Cailee Grace Shook, GA, Gordon Lee Memorial High School

Conclusion

When the last log dies into ashes
and even God, it seems, has fallen asleep,
Look to the stars and know,
there will always be a special place in my heart
prepared just for you, where you can bring your troubles
and lay down your weary heart.
Dwight E. Dieter, NJ, Editor

Inside of Me

to leave a loveless link

always save 2% of yourself
because you never know who will tear off their piece of you next.

where do you get off judging so many people?
for every sin you make—equates to a thousand papercuts.

twist the knife in my ribcage:
why do you think you're better?

he sets the standards
& crushes me with his all-and-nothing expectations

what's good enough?
i don't love you.

he nail digs in my chest,
a finger-sized hole named reality

burnt & engraved in my soul.
my eyes water with 2% salt

& with 98% regret
i walk over him,

turning the other cheek & avoiding his eyes;
respect me.

i only despise his imprints left on me;
yet i cannot fight my broken reflection.

so i let go.
& leave our loveless life behind.
Alice Tian, CA, The Nueva School

Cut the Grass

I am a child of weeds
Growing in the cracks of abandoned highways
The curve of my roots
Holding cracked asphalt together in a chokehold

I am hastily made
Meant only to spread my seeds and wilt
My flowers blooming
Only to be wrenched away by summer breeze

I am home grown
Begging for the pride of those who made me
Living a new life
Plucked from gardens I called my own

I am my future
Seen in the dewy dawn of Sunday mornings
But forever is a long way
For dandelion seeds to float
Alexis Barton, GA, River Ridge High School

when caterpillars become men

I am not ready for the day when caterpillars become men.

Though the ever-looming threat of metamorphosis is upon us,
I wish we could be as ignorant as when the universe was only
You, me, and the hungry birds above.

As larvae, you poked and prodded and pushed me off of my leaf;
I still wish I could fossilize our corpses forever,
Our ambition enveloped in amber, warm tones covering up aching bones.

You turned into a pupa without me ever realizing,
Putting up shields and inching away from me,
Pretending like I wouldn't notice or care.

Your chrysalis was hardened, now a dream which I could never pursue.
And sometimes, I still wish that we could be bugs once more.

Yet, you are molting,

Constantly evolving,

Changing into a man I've never known,
But one which I fear I've held too dear.

Despite your wings still sheltered by the wet, fragile chrysalis of boyhood,
I believe that it is now,

The day that the caterpillar became a man.

Ava Bunao, MI, Troy Athens High School

Driving is all the weight of adulthood

Driving is all the weight of adulthood crashing onto you at once
They tell you it's freedom, but ignorance is bliss
The passenger seat is a throne but the wheel is an obligation.
And really time is the same, it speeds up once your foot hits the gas.
A second ago, I was passing a stuffed bunny in the school parking lot
My mom was laughing as I painstakingly inched around it
Judgmental green plastic eyes worse than a traffic cone.
A second ago, I was passing a semi-truck in Atlanta, brow furrowed so hard
It made my head hurt
Every second sure I would hear the screech of metal and then nothing at all
I didn't die but I still feel like I should have.
A second ago, I was passing a patch of weeds in a perfect circle
And then stepping onto a humid rainforest of a parking lot,
Trying not to look up from the curb so I wouldn't have to feel small.
A second ago, I saw two headlights racing towards me…
And away…
Did they abandon me
Or spare me?
Sometimes I can't tell.
Gates Lilybet Jones, GA, Homeschool

Inside of Me - 41

She Knows the Future

She stands there

Alone

Her feet cemented
Into the gray
Thirsty ground

Reaching for her ankles
Praying on her tears

The smell of nothing
The sound of silence
The feeling of dread
Guilt
Regret

An empty void

With only memories
Of what used to be
But what can never be again

And all she can do
Is stand there

Alone

Julia Schlesinger, NY, Warwick Valley High School

Time Dreams

Time shifts strangely around me,
I look to the colorful walls of my prison.
Within this turning, shifting place I cannot flee,
I resign myself and watch the lit up prism.

It pulled time itself into the pyramid and sent streams into the world,
They hit the minds of a few.
Those with divergence were given time that's unfurled,
Internal clocks synced to something typicals never knew.

They see time in the colors they were given,
Not the completed white light the rest see.
Their concepts of time have been riven,
Those with divergence like me.

As I stare into the source of this difference,
And my mind starts to slip back away.
I'll wake up soon from this dream with no belligerence,
And live life the best I can with my altered day.

Avienda Margheim, SD, Vermilion High School

deconstructed sonnet to misogyny

It offers me a choice - descending as
a taut frame... *take the shape* and cave like clay.
Commended is my form, as harmless as
a whimpering cat, her claws clipped away.

Re*sist*, re*sist*, the plea resounds through me
But bones are brittle- fragments never quite
repair. When I refuse... *it shatters me*
i...

i SCREAM.
whydotheynotseeit
it is the *air*

        surrounding us every inhale we take
        is contaminated strangl*ing*drain*ing*kill*ing* the *life* in me

the ... exhales ... a ...
weak attempt to EXPEL IT

        it enters my throat swiftly choking me i can't breathe i can't speak I CAN'T SPEAK

    molding me pretty - it steals

all i am ... but mostly all i can be

I shiver at the haunting choice - which way
to lose myself? Predestined to decay...
Foram Shah, PA, West Chester Henderson High School

    Failure My Dear

    Your name is a curse on my lips, a sin strained behind clenched teeth
    The nagging voice of one so familiar and scolding hand that demands salute
    An ignominious crony that I had hoped to subdue
    My scheming accomplice—picking at long scabbed-over insecurities

    How haunting and eternal your cries seem
    I know you quite intimately—I cradled you soundly while silence eluded me
    Though you make me beg on my knees and fill me with a desire to flee,
    I acquiesce your companionship

    Failure, my dear, you are like liver and onions, Brussels sprouts and steak
    You are hardy, rubbery, and bitter to the point that I can barely chew, but
    You stay with me soundly and welcome me fondly, so
    I will try to embrace you

    Failure you get abhorrent reviews
    However, you are the only constant I can count on
    You are a friend who is always just an arm's length away
    You are proof that I did something, anything, and for that, I thank you
    Meigan Bailey, AL, James Clemens High School

New Beginning

These clouds never felt so low
This fog followed me with every footstep I took
I found it harder and harder to escape
And so I crumbled into grain

My weight so light that the wind took me in its path
I had no say in the direction I went

I had lost my sense of self
The same sense which had once pulled me
From the endless depths of my surroundings
But never had I been the thing surrounding myself

My lips brittle from the cold night
I felt the sun rising above my head
A new horizon had presented itself

The once boundless barriers of a broken mind
Had now become the almighty vast ocean
And like Moses had parted the Red Sea
I had parted ways with my doubt

In this time alone, She had handed me an answer

I was all that I needed

Jack Vaughn, NJ, Freehold Township High School

Like My Mother, I Am an Enigma

my mother speaks in slang and blues of her home
where grandma's rocking chair sits on the porch
and crickets sing in darkness among the tall grass
her words cascade down her lips and flow into my ears
she cries dried rivers
but yet
i drown myself
i inhale unbalanced vowels and respond in bursts of colors
pink
orange
green
her laughter rings of broken chords
sometimes i wonder if i'm a walking contradiction
i speak in movement more than tongues
while listening to the music of stomping feet that cleanses my soul
and try to perform the dances my colorful people have created
i smile
for a moment i hear a sound that feels like home
and i am complete.
J'Auna Demming, GA, Herschel V. Jenkins High School

44 –Inside of Me

Racing Thoughts

Run.

Usually, I refrain a moment to linger with my thoughts.
Yet my perpetual addiction to the short-lived dopamine rush overtakes me.
I inhale: my neurons push for stimulation, but my brain protests, upholding defense.

Run.

Prematurely I blunder, my body wins again - so much for mind over matter.
In a pitiful attempt to refocus, I begin to count my steps.
One, two, three...
But what do I want? What do I *desire*?

Run.

Is it too much to ask for peace, for comfort, for release?
My mind, multifarious, beckons for a chance.
When I strive for solace, it puts forth a will to mend.

Run.

And for now, I'm one with the grip of artifice
A delve towards introspection I must take
But what's a beacon of hope if not a facade?
And what's a second to dream if not a vice?
Carly Wytaske, MN, East Ridge High School

A Precious Heirloom

It is such a deeply troublesome thing to feel without being observed with no consequence of damnation, of the inevitable erring of ways.
What proof of life animates those pale and careful veins which never serve a guttural chuckle, a flush of full cheeks, a mouth filthy as a sailor?
One might speak of decadent and prized fruits, but these will surely rot if long coveted and never consumed.
Oh, what bliss! To be close to a thing as to consume it. To know it as well as its aftermath!
Only in finality can one understand the richness of experience, but then life is not to be contained in silly metaphors.
It is much more precious than the anxieties of those who ponder it.
And so I beg not to be slimy and scaled, pithy and stillborn.
Let me heave that first primordial wail of life: "Alive! I am alive!"
And I am in love with a million tastes and sounds and lights and colors.
I wish no reprieve- for at times I have laid warm in bed, I have seen the moon perfect and stained, I have held a friend, smiled at a child, nurtured a garden.
All along I have grappled with the sense of interwovenness that was only ever my own contentment, simply synonymous with the world's own.
I am glad that happiness is a novel of yellowed, calloused pages passed down by people I know I could have loved.
Rachel Kapllani, NY, Saint Anthony's High School

You Know

Sometimes I feel like my mom,
begging, begging, yelling, you know?
she worked hard, you know.
I get it now, you know?

"Use your words"
Well I do, but sometimes, sometimes
it takes hours, always hours for the sound waves
to bounce all the way to reach your ears.

"I didn't hear." Yeah. I know.

It's like swallowing sickness.
my turn, my turn.
It's a cycle you know?

I'm calling you now. Now, not later.
Get off the damn phone for a second.
I'm always second, you know?

I'm not mad though, you know?
you wouldn't know, though.
It's cause you asked me to do this,
but you always let the food get cold.
Lillian Newby, OH, Solon High School

Right Now

I'm staying
Staying up
Fingers on the keys
Shooting the breeze
Talking into the wind
In my mind
Quietly thinking of what is
And what has been
What could've been
Just a butterfly flitting in the air
A random thought
Turns into a string of curiosity
And I think
Of what could be
It's like
The magic string
Rolling through my thoughts
So I keep on
I think.
Ikeoluwa Esan, AZ, Hamilton High School

46 –Inside of Me

Waves, Snakes & Hawks

ANXIETY.
It comes in waves.
Pushed out + created by an unknown force.
Rising, tearing, then roaring and crying.

Nothing can stop it.
No one can hold out their hands to catch it,
Instead it slams down on the shore.
Instead it pushes through the cracks.

Over and under.
Side to side.
Anxiety finds a way in-
To stay and to hide.

Like a snake
Who sneaks around its prey.
Slowly and carefully enclosing in.
Until there's no room left to breathe.

Like a hawk soaring through the sky.
Soaring above all that is his.
Leaving nowhere to hide.
No place to call your own.
Alysa Kang, CA, Capistrano Valley High School

Petals of Violet

She swims in a sea of violet
The wind blows strongly yet quiet
A single rose desires wit
She waters it, she waters it

Water flows from pail to petal,
Washes down the stem to settle
At the ground as hard a metal
Elemental, elemental

The roots hold strong and supporting
In a dance the flower flirting
To a bee for its own hoarding
Never hurting, never hurting

As the flower still grows and blooms
The girl of violet decides to consume
All the loveliness of to whom
Something will bloom, something will bloom.
Lillian Boyer, IN, Terre Haute North Vigo High School

Birthday Candle

Papa,
I first understood you and mother through the flame of my birthday candle,
I was seven–the wax was sinking into soft, snow icing.

I closed my eyes tight and wished to be touched–
her firm grip replaced by cool fingers in my hair,
and *please give Papa the strength to extinguish.*

I mirrored you, then.
Eyes closed, one huff, another, *another–*
the flame refused to die.

On the fifth, a stroke of luck.

Fire became a stream of smoke, trying to reach heaven—*failing.*
It was frustrating, all-consuming, enough to make a man's breath cease,
and fathers are not meant to be food, but now it was ubiquitous:

Sometimes, all air can do is make fire dance.
Yet it is fire that needs air to breathe, remember?
Papa, you turn your back away from nature, so far away from weakness.

You nurture a fragment of hell so tenderly, so unapologetically.

Thuy-An Elizabeth Tran, CA, Piedmont Hills High School

Her laughs

Sometimes
her laugh is sudden;
an abrupt tear through the silence;
a rip in my ear.

Sometimes
it is warm; kind–
sincere.

And sometimes
It is mean. Cruel and curt
and cold.
Sharp–
It pierces my chest,
though muffled by the wall;
And I am but a casualty.

Yes there is a she
who is warm and full of love.
But I don't hear her lately.
Kaya Ilas, CA, Westridge School

48 –Inside of Me

The Influence of Aphrodite

My Lady Aphrodite
Your boundless beauty for all
Is needed once again
Teach us modern mortals the true beauty we hold

For while your statues have lost their color
Lacking golden hair, fair skin, and the fabric of your clothes
Maybe even some limbs
The things lost to time and earth have not diminished the beauty you are

Being no Victoria's Secret model
Your figure is one of health and indulgence
Showing that gain will never strip away beauty
And modern day has lost your knowledge of that fact

The oceans that birthed you knew your gift
Your ancient worshipers knew your gift
Your gift of unrivaled beauty
And the gift of knowledge in beauty of all

Return to us, and show us mortals a glimpse at ourselves
Of a beautiful figure without pains of illness and disorders
To show us every body is beautiful without need of suffering
I believe we need you again My Lady Aphrodite
Morgan P. Manning, CT, Lyman Memorial High School

The Sight

It happens every time the sun decides to rise.
Foot steps before foot as I walk into that all-to familiar room.
The eyes that belong to me see what they dread to see every single morning.
As they take in The Sight, my lips turn down into that o-so-repetitious scowl.
And then the uncontrollable thoughts rush into that brain of mine.
The Sight has too many imperfections.
The Sight has too many flaws.
All the eyes of mine can see are scars.

I imagine what it would be like if The Sight was different.
The eyes of mine close as The Sight appears in my head,
Only this Sight is flawless.
Imperfections vanish like the stars in the light of the sun.
Flaws disappear like the rabbit burrowing deep into its hole.
Scars are redirecting into that which resembles beauty.
Beauty like the sun crashing into the sea, spewing out vibrant colors.

But eventually those eyes of mine have to open up.
And that horrid Sight stares back at me.
My Sight.
The Sight of me.
Natalya Markey, HI, Abeka Academy (Accredited Homeschool Program Pensacola FL)

Inside of Me - 49

Thread

The precarious situation of distance
Like a thread strained from the pressure of lost moments
Held only by memories of before
Caught on one sided efforts and forgotten tears

The reeking smell of betrayal
For what is another name for simply giving up?
Because "forever" seems to hold no weight
And now the ends of the thread are frayed

From looking upon echoes of the past
Doubts invade the state of contentment
Until all that remains are anger and resentment

The push and pull to preserve and reserve
And the fleeting feeling of precious hope
But the claws of distance dig into this spot
Leaving pain within the absence

We watch as the thread falls to pieces
With stoic expressions and absent bodies
Becoming what we promised we wouldn't
For there are no more tethers, no more intertwined paths
Destined to forever float in opposite directions

Katelynn Robertson, OK, Bixby High School

Bye or Thank you?

I was standing at the bar, and a patron asked me-
"Bye. Or I should say thank you, I like both."
"Does it matter, sir?"
"Artless, you know what? Today-
I shifted from sad to depressed,
On a beautiful Sunday with empty candy shells.
I'm misanthropy,
It took 16 years to realize, then why do I just grin!
An imprudence voice told me that,
Hurry, go and look at your phone, then look at that album,
Oh, don't forget the mirror opposite you.
Listen, and repeat!
Sorry for the promises,
Sorry for the unwritten fabrication pages.
Just do it, do as I tell you.
My chest, my belly, also my eyes,
It hurts to the point of silence.
The only thing I hear from inside me, sorry.
But now, I was stubborn with the "two" at the beginning.
For not repeating, my soul will forever sob, like a curse."

Tuyet Kha Bui, CA, AIMS College Prep High School

50 –Inside of Me

Ink Parlour

Their hands were swathed in the layers of ink.
These are my hands, my strength, my power.

Is any being truly holy? Or simply imperfections of a Maker's vision?

Some of them have ink up to their shoulders, just out of the cooler.
The orange jumpsuits peak out of the plastic bags they leave in the front.
"A marker for my time lost, please".
Some of them are fallen soldiers, clouds swimming in their eyes.
Strong as iron, fortified with caskets beyond the brims of their minds.
"A marker for my time served, please".

They come in all shapes and sizes, all colors and sounds.
But they are us, and we are them.
They will rebuild, grow strong, and fall again.
Yet it is in the falling where our power lies and thrives.
For what are the hills, if not an answer to the valleys?

The eyes watching ourselves know only what we see to be true.
After all, who are we *but* judges?
I am only an inker. A listener. A storyteller. But I hear them with care.
For someday, I will sit feeble on the other side of this inking needle.
And I hope to God that someone will hear my story in their bones too.
Before Time marches forward to the endless currents of blue.
Nina Kini, CA, Valencia High School

Roses

When I think of bouquets,
I have dreamed of roses.
Much I marveled this posy flower,
it threw It's ghost against valentines
and its eyes had all the favoring.
I felt obliged to admire the vines,
I felt compelled to sniff the petals.
The stem held much power,
but in the fact that it was holding
such a flower.
Long I have stood there admiring its grace.
How could such a flower be in this place?
Like a jewel taken straight from my heart,
I crave every petal, every leaf,
every part.
But I'll grieve and I'll grieve,
to the trees and the bees.
Because I've dreamt of more roses,
than I'll ever
Receive.
Majesty Carpenter, TX, Arlington Heights High School

Inside of Me - 51

A Greedy Craving for the Void

Bliss is found where despair plays.
The discrepancy of it; ironically is comforting,
A hole I fall into and stay put,
For there is an exit, but I choose to linger.

Of all the choices, I prefer the worst;
It surrounds me in its exhausting warmth-
Ally myself with the pessimism and self-loathe,
It's a familiarity I'm unfit to let go of.

Maternal void controls the inhabitants,
Others grapple at its delicate insides to climb up,
But I revere it.
Saturate myself in pathetic self-pity,
With my back pressed against its ground,
Enjoying its heartbeat as my own.

I can choose to abandon the ache and forlorn land,
To own nothing but its residue,
And "get better".

Oh, but it's so delightful here!
I'll just stay put and watch you all above!
And subsequently dissolve into its pleasant dirt.
Huyen Amy Van Nguyen, TX, Eastland High School

Half a Conversation

Don't talk to me if there is a mirror around
I'll be too busy staring into my eyes
Not yours
Analyzing, critiquing, scrutinizing every scrunch of my nose
Digging into all my expressions
I rubberneck to see my reflection
Bending backwards to catch my gaze
Deciding if i fancy my features
Determining how beautiful I am
Correcting displeasing countenances
Til I'm satisfied with the result
Tweaking, adjusting, conforming just right
Yet it doesn't remain for long
My perfect mien trembles
Like a soft, gelatin mold
I attempt to set my face and hold...hold...*hold*
But I catch a glimpse of my work undone
Oh! The corner of my lip just out of place.
I will have to begin again! How embarrassing!
You've caught my vanity in full display
Clara Principe, AR, Mount Saint Mary Academy

Whispers Within: A Solitary Mind's Odyssey

In the silence of his mind, he roams,
A labyrinth of thoughts, a world unknown.
A canvas where his dreams take flight,
A sanctuary of ideas, both day and night.

He ponders the mysteries of life's grand scheme,
A tapestry of hopes, a whispered dream.
Each thought a star in his cerebral sky,
Guiding him through questions as they fly.

A symphony of memories, a sea of emotion,
He dives deep into his mind's boundless ocean.
Contemplating choices, paths not tread,
In the chambers of his mind, he treads.

An inner dialogue, a quiet conversation,
Exploring his desires and fears' foundation.
In the theater of thoughts, he takes his stand,
A solitary thinker in a wondrous land.

Unseen by all, he maps out his quest,
In the fortress of his mind, he rests.
A man adrift in a world of his own,
Thinking, pondering, seeds of insight sown.

Rayaan Seyal, CT, Fairfield Ludlowe High School

Bittersweet Lies

Her sharp words
leave behind a pungent taste,
like an orange peel
or tears when mourning
the loss of yourself

You squawk at me
with words of *love*,
but it remains salty
instead of sugary

Your apology
leaves me with a sweet tooth,
but turns me bitter

When will I learn
not to mistake—

Salt will never be sugar.

Derek Manahan, CA, Pinole Valley High School

Inside of Me - 53

Waterfall Feelings

I wish you could find me there.
Behind the solid wall where I hide
But everyone has a solitary space to spill out their despair.

You cross my path everyday completely unaware.
It is hard being alone across this divide
I wish you could find me there.

This feeling builds, but it's too hard to share
I'm full to the brim with pain and pride
But everyone has a solitary space to spill out their despair.

I see other people and try not to compare
Yet I get jealous and let that be my guide.
I wish you could find me there.

Some days I lose strength and feel far past repair.
It aches to think there isn't someone in whom I can confide
But everyone has a solitary space to spill out their despair.

I shout into the void a prayer
Over and over again, climbing up out of this hole, I've tried
I wish you could find me there
But everyone has a solitary space to spill out their despair.
Mackenzie Noelle Woyte, CO, Rampart High School

A Force of Nature

Writing.
A word with endless bounds of interpretation.
Its meaning is limitless, yet utterly simple.
In a sense, writing is...
a force of nature.
Words churn and melt into sentences
as molten magma stirs inside the trembling volcano.
Expression pours from the fingers that type;
speaking for the greatest depths of the soul.
A medium that flows from the mind
as streams of burning lava explode from the mouth of the tallest peak.
Ideas rush from every nook of the author's wits
with insurmountable force and speed,
leaving the crumpling ash of rough drafts in its wake.
Final revisions make their way slowly but surely onto the paper
as the last bits of viscous lava ooze onto land.
The writing is published, shared, discovered;
the effects of the eruption travel for miles.
Carried by the wind, the rain,
the writing.
Haley Branflick, NJ, Warren Hills Regional High School

Bonfire

A bonfire at their house
It should be my house too
But I feel far from home
When I'm around you.

Austic rolls in as I sit
Far away from the bonfire.
You're gathered round it with them
And you continue to get higher.

I hate to see you like this.
You have a sober soul.
But the drug that's called camaraderie
Has left a gaping hole.

Midding ten feet back,
I gaze up at the stars.
I always feel accompanied,
Doesn't matter how far.

I walk away, toward the street
And no one bats an eye.
Sometimes I feel invisible
So I never say goodbye.

Caleb Calkin, IN, Oregon-Davis High School

***

She had words on the tip of her tongue,
but they never made reality.
The road was clear but the door was closed,
and she was afraid to open it.

She had the power to create, but she held back,
her words piled up without meaning.
Bouncing like electrons, nowhere and everywhere,
Her inner thoughts began screaming:

Free as a bird,
I wish to fly,
but I am not heard, and
that door is why.

She had thoughts, but now they are lost.
They left with the birds in the sky.
Unless they are spoken, her voice will be broken,
and with it, her words
will die.

Carys Wiechman, TN, Fred J. Page High School

Why am I about to drown?

I'm about to drown
I'm completely spent
What does your mind revolve around?

That I feel like a clown
In a big red tent
I'm about to drown

I've been bound
In discontent
What does your mind revolve around?

That I've lost my crown
I can only lament
I'm about to drown

I've hit the ground
The goods been spent
What does your mind revolve around?

That I can only frown
There's bad all around
Why am I about to drown?
It's what your mind revolves around
Ryan Bates, TX, Kingdom Preparatory Academy

Leak

I leak the words of morning
But a sparrow I am not.
I'd rather be considered a frog, or even perhaps a moth!
This, my path to knowing
Clothed, my mind is not.
No? I've never heard that word.
What superficial talk!

If you want to rule the kingdom
You must first understand,
This kingdom does not hold a key.
(Not one known to man!)
So silly you would have a thought of a kingdom with a king
The brook would babble over him,
The bee would simply sting.

I gift my soul the sun, she needs it for her health.
I run until my lungs are lily's, help my brain is slugs!
Yet I'm content with all of it, this crass simplicity
But there's a leak in the faucet,
and I've gotta be home by three.
Elise Henry, MA, North Andover High School

56 –Inside of Me

The Eye of the Storm

I feel the ocean on my skin
I see the walls closing in
I stand in the darkness before the dawn
Here I am a helpless pawn
For I am in the eye of the storm

As the winds slowly starts it's advance
I fall quickly from my trance
The lightning strikes, then comes the thunder
My peace is quickly torn asunder
But I am in the eye of the storm

The ground falls and here I find
The storm was only in my mind
I take a breath, for now I know
That I will find my way back home
Away from the Storm

I wake again in a world like no other
The rains again begin to smother
The winds beat and follow behind
I, again, the storm does find
For I am back in the eye of the storm

Maria Jenkinson, OH, St. Francis De Sales High School

Icarus Unburned

As my fingers twist the bedside lamp to cocoon the room in velvet night,
stars line that smooth darkness, twinkling key lime green as they dance
across my ceiling in my mind.
It is a sight to behold despite the plastic that becomes so palpable
if I just rise and reach up to touch the glowing waxy cut-outs against
the popcorn-textured plaster above.

An Icarus unburned by the sun, I embrace this artificiality, for this sun
and these stars are an adorable facade, shining just for me.
How easy it is to not just construct a sky, but a whole universe.
I'd imagine myself a king, selfishly swallowing the wonders of the world
for my enjoyment. But even large celestial swaths cannot change
my fickle mind, always yearning for new creations to simulate and stimulate
when reality itself feels too dull and viscous to keep wading through.

To live amongst those false stars all alone each night
is to know the loneliness of the gods. I put them up, glued above my head,
so they would be the last thing my eyes gazed upon before the new day.
Their greenish bile-like glow mocks me. I didn't even get the color right
in my attempt to fashion my personal sky. Those stars snarl, whispering for
me to appreciate the real ones - stop sewing plastic into the fabric of my life.
Kings are fools, and I still covet like an Icarus unburned.

Ananya Balasubramanya, NJ, Cherry Hill High School East

Inside of Me - 57

Seasonal Depression

Months go by
And as the seasons change
As do I

September, October, November
First few weeks of class begin
I start to fall with the leaves

December, January, February
Days grow darker with time
I struggle to find warmth

March, April, May
Seeds sprout in the fields
I bloom with the flowers

June, July, August
Days grow longer than before
I shine with the sun

Months go by
And as the cycle continues
As do I

Angelina Holandez, NJ, Union County Academy for Allied Health Sciences

Invincible

Ascending through the air at elevated velocity
I felt the wind whirring on my wings soaring across the Earth protecting the nation
I wafted and billowed a stately and imposing sight
Up, up and over the blue and green terrene, the earth just a sphere

I understood all and nothing at the same interval
But, the bullets torpedoed through the sky and the blue twin-engine plane collapsed
Brooklyn Bridge severed like a white ring of tumult. The fragments pummeled down.
Skin and bones. I am a soldier returning harrowing, distressing

The slow descent through the sky falling, escaping, down, down
Into nothingness. The shrouds enveloping and swathing over me.
With nothing left but soot and ashes, a grotesque garden;
the questions are unfurled. The world we inhabit isn't always so kind

I have come to gain a peace of mind, and comprehend the meaning
Fighting to survive; the highs and lows, I'll be using and sinking into a haze
Lost and scared, and turning away as an unjaded wandering
In the hospital bed, I dream of yesterday; bruised and battered

A jagged scar already manifesting itself like a light switch stuck in the "on" position
A lifelong memory of the day that I was invincible.
Tucker Hankins, TN, Chattanooga School of Arts & Sciences

58 –Inside of Me

Air, The Unseen Soul Remedy

Anger, Frustration
Breath
Do you feel it?
Tears flowing down
Emptiness and chaos and rage and pain
Breath

Step out of the house
Be aware of your scenes
Touch...door
See...trees
Hear...birds
Taste...water
Smell...nature

"Let us spend one day as deliberately as nature.'
Oh Thoreau how I wish I could
To be one with nature not misunderstood

To be born in chaos
And rage in one to learn at that age
The purest thing I can reach air
It clears my head
Natalie Robinson, MP, Kubasaki High School

snowman story

making a snowman was always a chore
you had to get Mom to roll the biggest snowball
(really, she built the whole thing for you)
and it would always fall over a couple times
before it stood a little uglier than you had hoped

but still, you gave him an old scarf you didn't care about
and a hat that didn't fit anymore
and a face with a smile
borrowed from lost pebbles in the driveway
and it was then that he came alive.

looking back, the snowman wasn't happy.
the slightest force could have crushed his unstable body
and his brittle twig arms could, at any time, snap
admitting defeat to the unyielding siege of cold
it seemed he was always in a losing battle with his surroundings.

but then the next morning you go outside
and the snow has diluted into a murky slush
and you find all that's left of your creation
is a pebble-rock smile stirring in the water
and you realize you have made a self portrait.
Ayden Jantzen, TX, Aledo High School

Inside of Me - 59

The Dream is Questioned

When I was small
You were a part of my Sunday
The green and gold moving on the screen
colliding with other colors

As time past
I asked the most of my muscles
Grew stronger and faster
Became part of the whole
Followed the dream

The line
An immovable force
Challenges thrown at me
Strength tested against men
Endure the pain
Guard to protect

My blue and white
Clash against others
Covered with sweat and blood
The pain continues
The dream is questioned
Daniel Driessen, NC, Union Pines High

Cobs & Pens

Born ugly,
though deceptively charming.
Time persists, but no signs of aging
Erst a cygnet; gray and battered
Now pure, but not the Holy Spirit.

A liar,
though gloriously masked in white.
Yet, you proceed, seeking vengeance
Your black eyes beady
Your giraffe neck craned
Your hackles raised.

A mute,
for not a single song you sing.
Only a hiss remains,
but you're no serpent.

The little melody echoes
from the abyss of your breastbone.
You viciously flare your tongue
and give a sharp grunt.
Oh! must you be so cold?
Karolina Spiewak, MI, International Academy West

60 –Inside of Me

Raindrops for the Soul

I doubt our minds sleep
with our bodies

because mine never seems to stop
turning over itself

rain slaps tree leaves
as its remains splatter the ground

while wind cries out
colliding with glass panes

of course my weary eyes are blind to the battle
as twilight casts its shadow

in this case am i blissful
in my ignorance

or deprived of nature's beauty
as it hides under the covers

I can't see,
but I'll listen awhile longer.
John Cross, NC, Durham School of the Arts

Fight, Flight, Freeze in Giovanni's Room

I fight to push people away from me
    I fight for my isolation
        I then fight my own identity.

I take flight to escape my home
    I take flight to escape the trap that is my own body
        I take flight to escape reality by picking up a drink.

I freeze as a prisoner in my own body
    I freeze in Giovanni's room; "It's cold…Close the window"
        I freeze from the coldness emanating from my heart within.

I grow weak from all the fighting,
    raging to defend and define my masculinity?
I grow weak by the many flights,
    desperately withdrawing from reality?
I grow weak from the freeze,
    numbing me into apathy?

A physiological reaction that occurs in response to a real or perceived threat
    I bet against myself
        I prefer self-sabotage
I have never loved anyone? I am sure I never will?
Azara Mason, WI, University School of Milwaukee

Inside of Me - 61

Ghosts

I am a haunted house
the past lingering, never leaving
returning all the time, reminding me
of my sins. Cold hands, not
flesh, gripping my body, incapacitating me, rendering me to a
shell; trapped within myself, stuck watching the world unfold
around me. What is intangible controls me. Why
does it control me? Why do these phantom pains take away
rationality, leave me alone in the dark, living but not
breathing, asleep with my eyes open. Plagued with visions, restless
I can't move, disastrous futures, happier pasts
possessing my body, caging my mind. Specters lurk
in the corners of my vision, leering
patronizing, they see me, they tell me
I am
a vessel of the past
a fixed object, a dot on the map
haunted
Pahlychai Thao, OR, Oregon City High School

Words of the Winded

once, mother nature had built me out of her sticks, and stones;
constructing every one joint, and bone.
made only for her observation,
one never created for the taking;
but the wind then swept me away and now what will it make me?
I remember how I used to write with branches along the shoreline of blue water,
as it swept away every memory of my presence;
 and burned open wounds just enough to light a fire.
but now, there is only a surge of lightning striking in between my teeth.
of all the words I never spoke,
of all the ones I wish I didn't mean.
fighting me with every breath only to claw out of my blistered lungs.
I have always wondered,
what is the wind ever fighting for if not to be felt by someone?
Evangelia Mike, MD, Parkville High School

Beauty Standards

I fear that I lack the smooth silk of Beauty
Natural feminine features soft as dew on some Is
Hard and slightly distorted like the Red River Delta. What
Little joy and pleasure I get in my features is brisk. Until The
Disgust and hatred comes back steadily, like angry hail into my Heart
Quickly, I must cover myself like the ugly Christmas tree. My Makeup And
Necklaces are plastered on my bleak frame. "Oh how I look divine," I lie to my Mind
I replace my sour grimace with my daily mask, for its time to smile at the hungry dog I Chose
Laila Ward, FL, Booker High School

The Disappearance of Me

she understood willingness
and later the act of coercion
in the sense of when it applied to her
it was purposeful and in a way self-inflicted
like the wounds that later lined her arms
it felt calculated and sharp
I was there
I felt it
and I stood by
I was willing
or was I
was I not there
when I felt like I was in control
was my mind unconscious
had the feeling that I had lost
the most innocent parts of myself
sunk in
I finally the difference between being willing and being coerced
Jamile Molinero-Montiel, WA, Mead Senior High School

Offers Made to Prosper

Roaming through the land
The dire sacrificial lamb
Echoing free birds
Binta Bah, GA, North Springs High School

Purgatory

Religion is as foreign a concept to me as forgiveness
But in my darkest hour, I find myself on my knees
Hands clasped in a crude imitation of the devoted
Begging a being that I don't believe in to bring about the end
An end to this purgatory, this perpetual period of waiting
Mercy is unattainable for someone like me
But I find myself asking for just that
For the small kindness of hurrying me to my damnation
My lips stumble upon the sacred words of prayer
Making a mockery of the faith, yet I can't bring myself to care
I am too far gone, too jaded, too broken, too filled with self loathing
To recognize the perversion of an entire religion
Desperation has pushed me to desperate measures
I stay on my knees until I can no longer feel my legs
I continue to beg until my voice goes hoarse
I continue to endure this suffering
But unlike the last dregs of my faith, it never goes away
For this purgatory has no end
Audrey Malcuit, OH, Padua Franciscan High School

Maladaptive Daydreams

Look up in the sky and count the raindrops fall…
Soft in the moonlight,
there in the dawning valleys halos beam onto the soirées where everybody knows me.
For every cascade of our being in the sovereign blue silk, is a reason to stay.
The preponderance of iridescent bliss,
magic enlivens the soils from which the roses blossom.
The quant chills mist our skin and lift pixies to flight,
Long and laced hair now in the wind's braiding hands.
Every stone is embroidered in ivies, radiating a sense of nostalgia—
Or maybe it was the stream from the youthful waterfalls
 igniting joyous wonders of the future,
Where love is Shakespearean and life is euphoric.

A haze I'll keep in my mason jar
With the fairies still dancing inside
Every now and then I'll take the glass off the cupboard
Take a sniff—
A scent of happiness to forget reality.
Lainey Nicole Connell, LA, St. Scholastica Academy

>   overwhelming in great awe

                i cried when i looked at the stars
                its magnitude crushed me.
                and i realized

                i never did really look at the stars

        Kendall McKinney, TX, A&M Consolidated High School

        A diary's burden

        I rest upon your settled head
        Seek solace in the words you'd said
        Steward of straw, Trustee of thread
        Patron of pages left unread
        Your troubles served, My hunger fed
        Ears deaf from soundless shouts last pled
        I rest upon your settled head
        And dream of things I was instead

        Come back to me! And bring your woe
        So still you lie, and yet I know
        A part of you still thrives inside my tainted, tattered, tearing soul
        Your grief is now my own to stow
        Your perfect story mine to show
        The world will praise your beauty while
        Your ugly dies with me alone.
        Onyinyechi Obiakonwa, TX, Rowlett High School

64 –Inside of Me

Camouflage Bijou

They say beauty is in the eye of the beholder
Yet the gem was broken by the boulder
Who managed to cajole her and make her so cold?
The bliss of your breed is miraculous
It is almost as differentiable as calculus
She has always been fabulous
She glistened and began to walk
She listened and began to talk
She transitioned and began to flaw
What made her hysterical?
The pressures of the world cracked the gem
Was she ever enough to be fit for society?
Her beauty wasn't sufficient to fill the platter
Her intelligence was satisfactory
Her work was worth a fraction of a man's
Her worth could never be fulfilled
Until that stereotype was killed

Samantha Clark, FL, School for Advanced Studies-North Campus

The house in Which I was raised

I was born of hate
With guilt and grief sticking to my skin like birds to the sky
My mother cried on the day of my birth
So did I
I was taken from the safety I knew and brought into the cold shoulder of life
I was petted and kissed
Told I was beautiful and special
While I sobbed to the sound of heart monitors and the scent of blood and bleach

Emersyn Layton, UT, Brighton High School

To Be Just Me, Again

I can still feel you on my skin — now scrubbed raw.
Pink and fleshy
From trying to remove you.
My lips can still taste yours,
                      night air, and is that smoke?
    You taste like adventure, love.
  And I long for an adventure with you.
I sigh and brush my teeth,
again,
fighting the urge to coat my tongue in soap
just to get rid of you.
Too much pain.
Too much loss.
I wonder,
how to scrape my very heart clean of you?

Katherine Krugh, MI, Chelsea High School

Inside of Me - 65

What Can an Angry Woman Do?

I always seem to be the one in the wrong,
in your own eyes I do not know if you can see,
I am always the one to apologize.
Sometimes it feels like I am in disguise,
living a lie and you can tell,
because you know me so well.
So you yell so silently,
yet simultaneously loud.
With your motions you express your emotions,
so I reveal my side telling the truth,
not wanting to hurt you,
but yet it is still seen as abuse.
I am smart enough to see that I am not the archer currently,
but it does not matter.
I will still be pushed to the ground,
I am used and going to be reused...
until I bleed out.
Briana Chanel Samano, CA, Grossmont High School

Winding World

twists and turns
a winding world
winding down to a body full of curves
nothing ever lasts forever so enjoy it
the cycle of heartache
i *must* endure it

blue and black bruises on my ego,
on my esteem.
on top of the world one day
the next it isn't what it seems.
the world always turns it back on my body
why must i hush when i'm busting at the seams?
Sydney Speller, NC, JDC Early College High School

Those Dreams on the Shelf

There they sit- my aspirations collecting dust
Imaginations that may; ideas that might; desires that must

Ambitions I haven't nurtured
Due to my crunch of time
Visions I've seen but haven't progressed
Due to this life that isn't mine

Desires engulfed in excellence- unbeknownst but to thyself
Only left to rot at the expense of my schedule
There they sit-
Those Dreams on the Shelf
Jeremiah Vecchioni, WI, Bangor High School

When Cold Hands Touch

It's hard to find the right words to say.
When you asked me to come, I followed.
Not remembering your lifeless way.
Hands cold from my breath stung and hollowed.

A stranded passion with emotion on hold,
Expect my fading smile to return.
A lid encased our brimming fate, bright as gold.
Tingling fingers are eager to re-learn.

Patience waning, I ran to a distant home,
The faint calls and hope long gone.
Tears poured and remained, healed not by this poem.
Nails brushed back, the curtain long drawn.

Amelia Sommerhauser, AZ, University High School, Tucson

lineage

I know my mother,
and my grandmother,
but what of the ones before?
did they like to sing, as I do?
does our laughter sound the same?
where were my eyes from?
my hair?
has my face been loved for all this time?
will my soul?
who were they?

where will I carry them?

Charlotte Yih, NY, Hunter College High School

The Summer Before Senior Year

The sun's radiant beams encompasses me as I bask in its loving light
I soak it in like an unassuming sponge
It's all I can do to quiet the unwanted thoughts
In just six days time, school will resume
Gone will be the carefree days of childhood
Filled with laughter, amusement parks, and joy
In its place will be stress, college applications, and worry
The sun shines brighter, trying to cleanse away my struggles
It too knows that soon I will be too busy to enjoy it's warmth
In this moment, we are in ignorant peace
But the future is cruel and inevitable
A wistful sigh leaves my lips
As the sun's beauty breaks my heart

Oluseyi Oduntan, PA, Bensalem High School

Cheater

Ogling eyes and discreet glances
Small leans and shuffling shifts
On every word they wait, ready to pounce at even my unfinished thoughts
I feel the weight of their gaze, the scrutiny
Like a pride of lions observing a leopard with its earned feast
How hungrily they hang onto each click of my keyboard
How fervent their attention on my priceless work
How desperate their suspended fingers over their own keys
I try in vain to deter them, to pretend as if my mind is as empty as theirs
But it's not
Millions of fluorescent ideas engage me, itching to be released
But I must not give in, offer them what they vie for
I must not give them the answers
For when their work is submitted with my words, the grade reflected will not care for plagiarism
And my words will frown upon my traitorous actions
Because I've let the cheaters win
Katherine Larson, CT, Rockville High School

Two sides of the same coin

The void consumes life as it is undone
The bleak front brushes against the skin.
thoughts that linger are often disguised as one,
Our mind is a place of loose threads and ends
Our body is a place of affliction
Life as we know it through the aching heart
Amongst admission and recognition.
Pieces in the far are picked part by part
The vacant soul silently reshapes its mold.
Unable of stopping it, change has come
she runs and runs and runs and runs
grasping the hands as they start to unfold
Withholding the pressure that is, numb.
The void is filled and now all is blooming.
The back of my mind. You still consuming.
Dakota Warnsley, AL, Red Mountain Community School

Grief

My grief is not a montage.
My grief does not feel like a cinematic device.
It is not character development.
It is not making me stronger or better.
It is quite the opposite really.
It is broken sporadic breakdowns.
It is crying in the car with my mother
At the slightest glimpse of their past existence.
It is the little things that break me the most.
And it hurts more than anything.
Eva Wright, AR, Virtual Academy

68 –Inside of Me

Entry Denied

Why does a turtle hide in its shell?
You don't pose a direct threat and you haven't run at it suddenly
It would just rather be safe than sorry so it hides inside even after it knows you're safe
Because there's always a chance you're not

Why do mother bears attack anything near their babies even without immediate danger?
The cub is safe in a cave, you don't even know its there
and yet the mother runs out ready to attack
Ready to defend her helpless cub before it can be hurt
Before you can even get the idea

So why is it different when people act like this
You can't tell what the turtle has been through to be so scared
You cant see the cub
And yet these animals are reasonable

You do not know where I have been yet I am called unreasonable
You cant see the innocence i'm fighting to preserve so you call me unreasonable
Unnecessarily defensive like a frightened animal
So defensive, so scared
Yet they fail to realize
a frightened animal does not behave this way because its an animal
But rather because it is frightened
Eli Confer, NY, William Floyd High School

A Smiling Stranger

Every day that I passed the tree
It seemed as if her limbs extended further
Unapologetically she
took up space
Allowing golden light to paint her leaves

Despite her knots she stood tall and
smiled at the sky
she was happy
And it was beautiful

When asked who I want to grow up to be
Thoughts of this smiling stranger flood my mind... One day
I want to stretch my limbs as far as they reach
Feel the light painting my finger tips
Take up space and not be afraid to do so

Despite my knots
I will be happy
And I will smile at both my tree
and the sky alike
Only then
Will I be beautiful
Lily Collins, NJ, Paul VI High School

Inside of Me - 69

The pressure of being

The ocean is a body bigger than me
The waves, the tides, tsunamis, and typhoons could all kill me
Yet why is everyone pushing me to the ocean

The wind waltzes me towards its direction
Old friends resurrect to push me into its waters
Family do not quite understand the turmoil I'm in
Whether I'm okay or drowning
They seem to push me as if they don't know any better

The ocean must be calling my name
The way it walks and talks is the same way I do
Its power isn't its own
The moon, the earth, the air
The more control they have over the ocean
The more it wants to break free

The ocean and I are the same
A trap I might be falling into
Perhaps at least with the ocean, I will feel at home
I walk in, without hesitation
My steps, languid, soft
My mind, tumultuous but finally at peace
Brevia Kibet, AL, Mobile Christian School

The Chapel Window

I think I see a face in the stained glass window.
Oh, what terrible expression shades his visage.
Age has done him cruelly, experience has invited sin and doubt.
Doubt! In a holy place such as this?
This man has started to shatter, and salty tears fill the crevices.
Vices, such as his, fit in only with crows;
Woes of man have no place in this clean cathedral.
All this space, but nothing can be spared for one who is less than perfection.
Perfection is the glass mosaic that lays over his sinful face.
Facing the window, closely critiquing the figure, I realize he is only my own reflection.
Izabel Wilson, UY. Box Elder High School

i have known the moon

the summer sun sinks into the sea
taking the glimmer of my love with it.

when the warmth in my cheeks is overtaken by the pale night
when the ocean's soft breath makes my soul shake and shiver
when frigid water rises and beckons me to come over. to give in.

i'll remember that the blue was always there

Victoria Heng, CA, Long Beach Polytechnic High School

70 –Inside of Me

I Am

I am from a paradox of stars, the moon so bright,
sometimes illuminating my future path.
I wonder when it will be my turn
to shine as bright as the stars.
I hear the sound of my own voice
telling me I must make my family proud.

I am from laughter and sadness being my only two moods,
I am from leaving my salty tears on my pillow to letting go
and moving on. I am from forgotten memories and hurtful words.

I am healed, no longer vengeful or regretful.
No longer focused on my past, but my present
and future, that's looking bright.
I am from the friends that are now family
and the blood that is no longer family.

I am from the smell of books and words written on
the pages, them being my escape from reality.
Tear stains soak the pillow as I worry of who I'll become
when I'm no longer the person I hope to be.
I am the best version of me, the one I've fought so hard to keep.
I am me.
Lily Berzoza, CO, Westminster High School

Collide

When it was over
I watched the sun collide with the stars
A perfect balance of uncertainty
But her beauty remained

Is apocalypse a moment?
When the sun shown just for a second to humor the coming darkness,
Or to remind us that there is more than this fleeting moment?

I see you in every passing car
Stare at the pictures, but I have too look to hard
When the birds sing, they don't sing for me
Should I act surprised, when you'd rather be without me?

Now the distance is gone
But you're just as far away
And I'll wait in my head
Every moment of every day

Your love is a dam
The river won't flow
And when the sun rises again,
Will anybody even know?
Gavin Martinez, CA, Vista del Lago High School

Inside of Me - 71

Lord of Larvae

I can feel the whispering of hornets in my ear and the song of the cicada,
The chirping of crickets and the hum of the bumblebee.
My flesh becomes a safe ground for the pupa of moths and butterflies,
But my skin stretches and hardens like the armor of a beetle.
I feel more akin to an insect than a human now.
My arms have become bent, pointed, and sharp,
not refusing to hurt any cockroaches who come near me.

The depravity I was exposed to have left me a shell of myself.
I am only worth the same as maggots crawling in the rotten flesh of a corpse
Or the larvae of flies who have driven themselves into the decaying scraps of food.
Looking back on myself is a longing I will never be rid of,
The image of me now is only a bruised and beaten child.
What they wanted me to be was a beautiful luna moth.
But I turned out a mantis, and I will bite off the head of anyone who hurts me.

I was sent crawling to an early grave, peeling off skin for my delayed metamorphosis.

Max-Ryker Sparks Simpson, CA, Jery and Gary Anne High Tech High School

Dyslexia

Seeing words sdrawkcab and forwards,
Switching words in brain your without you it knowing,
Having to duoble check every word you spel,
And having to double check every word you pro-noun-ce,
Seeing words differently than everyone, and not realizing.
Having to stress about reading out loud.
But you have to keep it a secret.
People thinking you're stupid,
But they simply don't understand.
Reagan Graham , NV, Spanish Springs High School

Santa Barbara

From your rock garden,
I steal away with a whisper--
for sunlight spares no warmth
on the damned.

Over ugly pink water,
the drunk mist heaves through.

I've watched us change over
these bitter moons; together,
our sweat still smears and boils raw
under sweet lies & grazing storms.
Sienna Smith, NC, Croatan High School

My Anxiety

It's subtle, the way she enters the room.
I'd lay there, unseeing, unthinking.
And she would fill the space between my arms, on my chest,
silent, yet shattering as the cut of a train on its path in the night.

My lurch, and pulse races into the space before me,
its beating drum floods my room,
loud with the sound of my fan and my heavy heart.

My chest heaves under the weight and my breath flutters,
I struggle to catch it, aflight before me,
it loops unbound and, in a moment, the fan whisks it away.

My thoughts, they darken,
my eyes see not my room, but my memory,
they see you, but not as yourself.

You are a dark figure, a shadow in my doorway.
You are a hand creeping around the edge of the doorframe,
And you are sad, you are mean; you are unlike yourself.

And I know it's her that brought you here, but she's so quiet,
all she wants is a place to rest.

And I cannot turn her away, cannot lift her weight off my chest;
so smothered by the train tracks and the drum.
Brooklynn Wolfs, KS, Blue Valley West High School

Nothing But

A girl is nothing but a person
A mistake is nothing but an event
Words are nothing but the past
Life is nothing but a test
Some would attest that it's a journey
But I would say I'm still learning
I'm nothing but a girl
Who makes mistakes
And speaks a tongue of honesty
And lives to experience
Longing, yearning, and always wanting
Hurting, enjoying, and always living
I'm everything and nothing but a girl
Just a person
Who isn't perfect
But is making their own way there
Brazil McNeal, CO, Thomas Jefferson High School

Inside of Me - 73

the silence is deafening

the perfect memories: a broken frame,
sweet night, she knows it all; for they know naught
of distant voices, calling out my name,
and yet 'twas I who built this cage, was it not?

or was it the despairing ghosts; mindless drones,
amidst the empty faces I walk among,
the same, yet nothing alike; hollow clones,
the tragedy of song too early sung

a tale that's not yet told; I ask the night,
where have the fragments of my dreams hidden?
for I know not, neither does she; in spite
lives in the shadows, lurking unbidden

and slowly, softly, I fade away as
the blind world goes on, like it always has
Hanaa Farooqui, CO, Rampart High School

NUMB

Fatal silent death
No tears as you play-out your fears
Desperately trying to feel whole again.

I feel as if I am not real
My mind used to constantly talk
Which would lead me to gawk at the emotion
That would surface

But now I feel none.

I finally know what it feels like to be
  N
    U
      M
        B.
Emma Walter, PA, Williamson Jr/Sr High School

Awake

How barren is consciousness when residing in a place forlorn,
A chasm that echoes into perpetuity as the wind in its decadence adorns,
The faded walls, a distant allegory that reminds the masses of a cave,
For all to look in and judge this place that even the strongest dare not brave.

But when spellbound merchants in starlit cloaks come in the gossamer night,
Those who create dungeons for their wandering minds no longer cower out of spite,
And the untethered beauty of the universe is released where in mere moments one can explore,
What was, what is, and what will be as a thunderous ocean washing inexorably upon the shore,

The cavernous chasm is gone, not for the ignorant, but for the wise,
The aware who with intention see it is only the empty who grasp at that shapeshifting guise,
Which takes away life's unadulterated claim that the decomposed soul must compose,
Those ink-stained words of a scintillating future that possess the exquisite meaning of prose.
Annabella Rose Soldevilla, FL, Miami Arts Studio 6-12 at Zelda Glazer

74 –Inside of Me

The Grand Stairwell

the stairs will crumble as you step
they'll feel the burden all except
the ones who wait for you to fall
don't mind their souls
forget them all

just carry on, the world won't wait
for your success to change their fate

some won't know
how far you came
without their help or crushing tame
you'll look back down
the grand stairwell

and watch its victims
they'll rebel
some may fall and some may conquer
if they persist, they'll get to wander

no need to grieve the journey here
for it was tough and they could see
the only thing you need to mourn,
is how naïve you were before
Jocelyn Valentin Reyes, CA, Baldwin Park High School

Circling Back

There we are, alone in this place we call
Home, is where the heart is, where is my
Heart? I lost it back there, along the winding
Lines, they lead me to nowhere, to an old
Memory, so glaring, so ugly, I'd rather forget.

When we try to walk away, can we really
Walk away?, who would want to leave? they
Ask, and we'll tell you, but you won't really
Believe, focused on each, new prolonged
Day, away from home, those you want to remember.

Now, I have all these thoughts, but few seem
Mine, such a mangled thought, forcing a great
Pause, think of where we've been, where we will
Be, just exist for a while, escape from the
Mind, and then, we'll end up here, alone.
Abigail Garnica, CA, Rancho San Juan High School

Behind Locked Doors

Obscured: Can I be trapped in a place where I placed myself?

Careful, I close the door, "To keep others out or to keep me in?" and reach the lock- "To exit, someone else must make an entrance."
I could be free but at the high cost of exposure, and money does not grow on trees.

Relief is autonomous as she flies in. Like a pesky mosquito, she drains the warmth from my body as the cool, crystallized porcelain numbs my ready skin, thus generating the sluggish pumps of my leaking heart, becoming a reminder that my body is simply a breathing corpse. I feel the physical matters, but the things that would matter don't and are instead muted, heavily diluted. I see the spattered bathroom mat, a prison-cell gray- dull, dead-staining and stained with a fuel I can expertly conjure and control. It arrests the dreary rug into coalescing from its bleak state to tones of rose and sepia as it dries-now an elixir of refreshment and remembrance.

Groundbreaking: It hits the ground; it breaks a heart, perfunctorily participating with egregious execution on my part. I serve myself a slice of cake only to feast with my eyes. Then it ends- the horror film. I watch to see the light flood in, sharp-edged and jarring to dark and desolate-adjusted me. The credits roll, and whispers of "drop it" reverberate off the lifeless walls, barely audible, yet deafening in the intensity of the silence that I could hear my pain drop. An arrogant serpent hisses in the shadows; it echoes and remains, eliciting sweet sounds of dissonance as it clashes with my willing accomplice, who retreats to the bathroom floor, leaving trails of scarring evidence alone with me. I appear solely guilty. What more can I do?
Behind locked doors, it pours.
Briseis Bradley, VA, Grassfield High School

After the Storm

I've found a way to use the crickets.
The hedge needs trimming and the trees don't fit,
but the chirping crickets and the autumn breeze
bring a scene that's worthy of Shelley.

I tried the trees alone, and the hedge,
for what it's worth, but I could not write it.
The sirens on the interstate, and the words you sent
through Ma Bell, the ones which sit at the pit
of my stomach like the bad news that they are.

It's true what the radio says, and my father,
who never trims the hedge, and the old lady,
who lives on the other side but only comes out
on Sundays to water the flowers.

The world probably never turns, and nothing ever changes,
except the darkness, and the trees will never fit,
and the crickets can sing and sing forever,
but the hedge will always need trimming.
Dwight E. Dieter, NJ, editor

MY World

What Happens

To dreams left unfulfilled?

Starved and macerating in time, until they shrivel into bones—
Six feet under, in the musty maw of sediment,
Satiating its own hunger— decimating and digesting
In the jaws of the dirt; their conception but an eventual offering
To the stone and flower-riddled turf.

Or do they fly, fly until they can no longer bear it;
Fluttering like a heartbeat; relentlessly—
Pulsating against the cerulean blue tile of open sky—
An unearthly clatter of wing bone and glass tile— an unsettling silence
Like that of a whisper, daring to be extinguished from its lips.

A smattering of arrows— those dreams left for execution—
Forever chasing the pummeling blood, gurgling with life and potential,
Churning and— babbling with a mineral viscosity
Parallel to that beneath the feet.

Sharp and tumultuous with the desires that rake from inside it,
Breaking through flesh, through organ, through heart— in attempt to fly,
Like arrows cast down from the punitive sky.

What happens to dreams left unfulfilled?

What happens to their victims?

Corinne Sherwin, NC, Panther Creek High School

A Narcissist's Failure

ailments straight from the sun
nihilists gather to scream under the moon
am i just an extension of your emotions?
rally together and defy everything we promised to love
collective, they lock us in our mirrors and ask what we find
inside? do you even care what's inside
searing us with brands from the top of the chain
sit and watch as our heads melt on the pavement
it could never be as we hoped
so that even the narcissists from the stars could not protect us
that our lovers from the end of days could not define us
sweet child, open your eyes and look up
fold your heart deep into your chest and never let them see where it rests
and if they ask who you wanted to be, smile and pretend not to hear
if you should fly, let it be in your dreams
love before it is too late
unto us, they have burdened the world
reap our souls into the net until we can learn how to hold them
eyes closed until it happens all over again
Anousha Baqai, CA, John F. Kennedy Middle College High School

Acculturation

In an exotic scene of a room filled with stacked moving boxes, pitch of
quietness, lack of fresh air, and dim damp smell thrusts her senses.

Father smiles at his daughter: *"This is our new home."* She thought
the place resembled nothing of her home: *This is and will be no shelter.*

The glimmers shining in her role model's eyes outrun & engulf the words
in her throat. She ate her stories of embarrassment from broken & foreign

accent, exhaustion from hearing her name ruined by aliens—who reside
in the place where he calls home—then again, an awkward rise of volume

of her cheeks & exposed teeth hope to obscure true intentions, attempt to
imitate the same excitement & delight, in exchange for her embarrassment and

dismay. She ate her fears of inciting a catastrophe when the aliens reproach
her, as her name is Hongju, not Mary; her food is tteokbokki, not Big Mac.

Eaten fear diminishes into crumbs. That my mien, story, and voice is home.
Home is and will be no dull.

My shift of hues & homes will blend into a certain pattern. Underneath
discomfort find comfort. Only so, clumsy and earth-covered grace is peeled

off from obsolete silence. I joy with an elemental smile.
I scribe my America.
Hongju Cho, NJ, Tenafly High School

A Vast Sea of Possibility

The sand pokes the soles of millions, treading slowly under the vast sea.
Inside the sticky sandals and glistening eyes of a smiling little girl
Touching it as small dots crawl up and surround her knees and arms.
The familiar aroma of the salty sea
carried around the bright rainbow umbrellas and ice cream truck
Songs of childhood and pure delight in the cool summer breeze.

Breathlessness to what was before her: a vast expanse
Possibility for more and a stirring hope.
Each step came with an angry sharp glass hidden in the sand
Before the bone-chilling waves pushed her back to shore
into the dots. They grabbed and held, unknowing of what lay ahead
for the little girl.

A vast sea of possibility.
Those little dots held on tight, restraining
Scared, anxious they all were
For the uncountable paths there lay
But to the unknowing, hopeful eyes, there were only dreams.
Rexana Chen, NY, Stuyvesant High School

I, too
An inspiration by Langston Hughes

I, too, sing America.

I am the image of divine femininity.
I stand at the face of society
Bearing its judgment of my choices
But I stand tall
Never breaking a sweat

I hold the burden of balance
Perfection
I calculate the course
Of my every action

I Smile! But not too big
In fear of sending unintended signals
I Speak! But not too loud
In fear of becoming a nuisance

I Flourish
In the devineness
of my woman hood.
The power of my distinct nature
unwavering.

I, too, am America.

Meron Aman, NV, Spring Valley High School

Grieving Red Hand

When I was younger, I knew that I was Native;
Growing up, I realized I have yet to find out what it *really* meant.
However, America taught me
—it means *grief.*
I am engulfed in *suffering*,
Every day, we are *beaten, murdered, raped, kidnapped.*
And it could be my grandmother one day,
my sister the next,
me, shortly after.
I could be one of the many *missing* and *murdered*
and there will be no one looking for me except for my family;
and when they discover my remains,
They will *grieve with the Red Hand atop their mouth.*
They will realize it is not *our* hands that are red,
but it is the hands of those who took *everything* away.
And so, I *grieve* with the Red Hand splattered on my face,
because America has belabored the point that
—being *Native,*
means there will be no justice served.
Stephanie Job, CA, Francisco Bravo Medical Magnet High School

Միութիւն

I trade my LA shirt for your Lebanon headscarf
You trade your Kuwait uniform cord for my USA long-sleeved
We trade snapchat codes and instagrams
Trying to quickly tie ourselves together
Before commercial airplanes traveling in opposite directions tear us apart

It was so easy meeting everyone and becoming friends
We were all meant to love each other
We just didn't know it until we first shook hands
Until we first exchanged smiles
Until we first sang Gini Lits under the victorious downpour of the rain
With the powerful beat of the drum bringing us closer together as brothers and sisters

And we smile because we know that the Armenian spirit still burns strong
The scattered shards of pottery have been temporarily reconstructed
And the vase is more beautiful than it was before it was broken
It is our hot blood and passion that holds it together
And it is our love for each other that makes it beautiful

And so it hurts me to leave my newfound family
Taking with me only memories and a wardrobe from around the globe
But I take comfort knowing we will see each other again
միայն ցտեսութիւն
Sevan Cash, CA, California School of the Arts -- San Gabriel Valley

*Translations: The title means "Union" and the last line means "only goodbye"

The Whale

Vast, unending, the glistening body of water continues its grace
Laughter echoes, smiles reflect from all, as the roaring wave befriends
Yet, in solitude, she remains, strangled, unable to escape its embrace
Again, and again, last breath exhales, and she descends

Consumed, alone, she longs for comfort, the tears of the sky
Instead, confirmation echoes, in isolation, reflecting the desperation
Ink paints her canvas, pitch black, blinded, all below die
Then is marked, the unending difference, her separation

Her confusion lingers, the difference from others, the rejection
Liveliness vibrates the surroundings, just enough to taste the bitterness
Lost, resentment remains, the questions of why, the imperfection
Cursed, forever, nothing changes, the world didn't hide its wickedness

Unlike all else, her home was nowhere to be found
Wandering along, realization strikes, the midst of all torment
Undeniable descent, plummeting, yet she never drowned
Oh, so different, yet similar to others, how all seemed to comment
Lovely whale, may you rise, and fall, and comfort, as it was, and is
Angie Minjung Kim, CA, Gretchen Whitney High School

Staring Contest

This is the story of a little girl who sat on her mother's lap on the Emirates plane
as she had a staring contest with the city lights below her
"C'mon, I'm only five, let me win!"

They seemed nothing like what she remembered from Bangladesh merely hours ago.
They gleamed at her with opportunity.
With hope.

The clouds bounced around
                      rearranging   themselves
          into   shapes
                    that made the   little girl smile

The Tall Skyscrapers, The Stubby Green Trees, The Zooming Yellow Taxis, The Spacious Stadiums, The Brick Of The Bridges, The Clutters Of Buildings called for her

She'll be the first to experience everything from scratch.
The first to go to elementary school in America.
       To high school.
           To university.
                She will run, so her children and their children can walk.

Being the first to it all makes her who she is today.
Her work ethic is driven by her desire to make that little girl, who sat on her mother's lap on the Emirates plane as she had a staring contest with the city lights below her, proud.
Mosammad Khanom, NY, Stuyvesant High School

On hearing the bus park at my stop...

Exasperation sighs,
Signaling my release
Of the pent-up, the fed up
                    Exhale.
Screeching of the joints,
Strenuous swell suffocating,
Breath pulled taut from the hefty
Sum of our worries,
The brink of *break*
                    Exhale.
It sighs.
Releasing a breath
Releasing the bearing of the mass,
Our mass,
Of the day's burdens
                    Exhale.
I feel light
When I fumble down the rows,
A skip to my step
Carries me home.
       Yasmina Haddad., TX, Cypress Woods High School

82 – My World

stripped

we sit still, stay silent
our eyes lay unshining.
we are stripped bare,
and we bear it.

we follow every direction
with practiced perfection.
but our unfailing obedience
is simply seen as deviance,
it holds no significance.

we do everything we are told.

yet stygian swords still slice our souls,
whips of words will wound our worlds,
brutality beats us down till we are bruised and broken.

We will not let this stand.

It is a great, unjust war
Terrifying, yet a cause worth fighting for,
We stay unyielding until society is at its knees
Crying with pleas for mercy.
For the light of its cruel beauty
Will rain down upon this earth.
Karishma Pilla, TX, R.L. Turner High School

Nail Bar

white fluorescent light
complimenting gray drab walls
lined with a nail polish rowhome
of every color present for the imagination,
but not so for the dreams of the immigrant
mother working at your extremities
for sustenance rather than an
aptitude for buffing tips so
below the pedicure chair
her cracked earth hands
massage your calloused feet and
purifies them with a polluting acid
then summons flowers on your nail beds
in a longing to rest on them
but "Sorry, sorry" she says
so you will tip her well
because she is here
caring for the lowest part of the body
cultivating your high-handed beauty
at the sacrifice of her own
Jennifer Tran, PA, Central High School

A Faint Summer Morning

My tumefied eyelids crack open, the genesis of dawn tastes near–
disguised objects line themselves, conferring as if they were wed,
while dark threads dance around my bleary peripherals.
The space around me foreign yet homespun–
colors combine to muddy hues,
objects conjoin in amalgamation.

Sound like heavy tides, seduced by the crescents' bequeathing.
Mother Nature thrums in chirps and squeals,
the quiver of pinions neighboring as verdant clusters of leaves encase husk lumbar–
towering over the bristled grassland, glazed by the morning's chill tears.

Imperceptible blustery pushes against the palisade,
its dubious gesticulation–like spirits–
brush against my warmth mumbling "ooooooh",
collecting subtle shudders from me.

Her warmth reaches out to my tissue, trailing quills of bumps– I recoil.
She gleams in response, ever so golden, pendulous from heaven.

These bearings ceaseless,
yet never breed tiresome,
nor tedious.
It is this routine that makes me covet such summer mornings.
Nikole Brodsky, KY, Bourbon County High School

Where I'm From

Where I'm from,
the grocery list has a monthly limit where milk is never the priority to
our growing bones,
unless covered by the fees of another man.
I'm from where the worn wood and grime meet.
In our neighborhood, lives are shackled to the burden of learning until
we can get out and no longer
Be where I'm from.
Where I'm from no one can see their destination or know when they'll leave;
we can all only hope to make it out.
around here feels like my one sixteenth birthday wish to for a pair of
shoes that aren't two years worn,
I'm from where the cars don't run on nothing but weekly earned wages and a prayer
the car doesn't stun.
It's embarrassing to ask around for assistance,
so we flaunt what we don't have.
Here birthday cakes are poorly frosted and made by one's own love.
where I'm from I wonder if I could make it big one day like the girls I see
out of our old television set,
If only it didn't matter where I'm from.
Araylia-marie Martinez, WA, Kalama High School

Eternal Embrace

In whispers of twilight's embrace,
Words dance upon the canvas of space,
A poet's heart, a soul's reflection,
Ink spills, an artful connection.

Lines drawn from dreams' elation,
Mingling with imagination,
Stardust woven in every verse,
A universe, a breath, a curse.

Eyes glimpse the world through poet's gaze,
Unraveling life's mysterious maze,
With metaphors, they paint the skies,
Unveiling truth, where beauty lies.

In syllables, emotions soar,
A symphony, forevermore,
Through highs and lows, they navigate,
In poetry, they find their fate.

With ink-stained fingers, they create,
A tapestry of love and hate,
And in this sanctuary they dwell,
The Live Poets Society, where stories swell.

Quan Do, CA, Mira Mesa High School

Always?

Always taking
Always giving,
Always there

Sending rain to help them live–
And swirling storms to drown them
Always there

Growing plants to help them breathe–
And wildfires to make them stop
Always there

Giving them the highest peaks and the lowest trenches, wonderful–
And the wonders killing them if tempted
Always there

Letting them use the world–
But too much
Mother Nature's always there
And now she's not

Mehul Pahuja, TX, Frisco High School

11 AM Matinee

Everyone's a midwife in a movie theater

For two hours AMC attendees are like
Budget exorcists and their subjects

Both have demons it's just that
The willingly exercised can still feel them.

From two to whenever reasonable movie duration time:
When the beloved trailers run
One, into the next:
A band of ushers files up the rows
Standing   in   the windows
Between   each   seat
Making a painless incision on the chests
Of Paddington six preview enjoyers
Unaware that above their ribs the little plum
Now exposed to the open air
The problem organ glows and ripens

Like turning the oven light on
Suddenly some tired group of cattled people
Their beating is synching
And you can find a pulse

Liv Amiri, CA, Crossroads School for Arts and Sciences

Hush...

The hazy amber streetlights dim as crisp maples waft onto your windowsill.
You wonder why they twirl in and detract away like everyone you've known.
Lukewarm air from your heater brims your lungs to your mind with ambiguity;
triggering playbacks of ecliptics, hunting your will of righteousness.
Did your foe forsake their wrathful tapestry wrapped around your shoulders?
Does your crush recall his heartbeat during your timeless gaze?
You restlessly toss and turn while the metronome amplifies your pulse.
You swoon your soul into the '90s floral pillow,
praying that the moody mirrorball halts its hypnotizing crimsons and jades.
Your parents conveyed that the capital has vivid potential,
but high-rises don't veil this town's howling hounds or hopes.
Swift moon phase shift, now you're in the spotlight, crippling;
Though a celestial essence elucidates the fog in the azures of many.
Its embers ignite blood flow to your frostbitten cheeks,
and the once estranged flame in your pale pupils.
"It's not your fate to combat clashes, salt your gashes,
and pierce your puerility," it assures.
And when you reach out the window, you feel one with the erupting monsoon.
And when the stars combust your chains from exile, the sparks spell out:
"Hush. You survived."

Riddhi Sharma, CA, Evergreen Valley High School

86 –My World

Dammed River

Held by chains much too long, about to burst
River caged, River shunned, her power schemes
Destruction is foreseen, expect the worst

The walls grew slowly, not noticed at first
Freedom flickered saving most, while others screamed
Held by chains much too long, about to burst

A crack keeps the walls from being immersed
Her vigor could drown cites, whole regimes
Destruction is foreseen, expect the worst

Crushed by the weight of a thousand mounts cursed
Her life a struggle, tearing at the seams
Held by chains much too long, about to burst

A time soon the sad world becomes many streams
Her streams, sprinkled with signs of ruin, gleams
Destruction is foreseen, expect the worst

Welcome these words, for she is not the first
Thoughts imprisoned are as trapped as her streams
Held by chains much too long, about to burst
Destruction is foreseen, expect the worst
Ileri Babalola, TX, Early College High School

Lights

Once it finds its way to the wheel
The hamster wheel, to keep going
It's captivating, adrenaline flowing
An endless cycle of want, of goals that never
Stay fulfilled

To come and make them yours
All the wishes that you never made
To see a sun with rays of ambition,
A moon with stars of souls you've helped
A dream of years like honey

But we keep running, on a high line
Tile by tile we see it narrow
Of gray levels and gray skies
We reach, in hopes of color
Of dance and music, of eyes on us
We seek a little smile at the end of the day
That can tell us we've done it,
Under all of our lights; but instead we
Keep seeing gray.
Ananya Vuppala, NJ, Marine Academy of Science and Technology

My World - 87

Rivers of Ink

In the quiet corners of a solitary room,
the lamp paints shadows in its gloom.
My heartbeat, a drum, syncs with the ink's drip,
a dark river carrying tales from my grip.

Memories heavy, love that burned too bright,
pain that lost the way to fade in the night.
All seeping from my gin-soaked marrow,
each stroke, each word, a whispering sparrow.

Night deepens, hours unwind into a spiral,
laughter, now a distant echo, seems almost viral.
Silence under broken wings, a haunting song,
all bleed into this river, stretching long.

This river, a mirror of hidden life's gambles,
an open wound, ceaselessly bleeding, it rambles.
Seeping into the parchment's unending thirst,
an immortal dance at life's crossroads, rehearsed.

Such is the fate, a scribe in the night,
his only company - shadows and the moon's light.
In the dance of ink and drink, he sways,
his river, a pathway to unwritten days.

Sean Burns, NJ, Sayreville War Memorial High School

Trapped
Inspired by Claude Monet's painting "Rocks at Belle-Ile, Port-Domois (1886)"

Each particle of sand reminds her of the stars in the sky
and the wave crests which look like the moon.
Unexplored, she resonates with the calamity of the sea.
If she touches the water, her life is over;
if she walks away, she cannot breathe.
She is the ocean. The water reflects
her soul with its motion.
Her eyes are cloudy but not because of the sky.
Jagged shells reveal themselves as the ocean pulls away.
Hypnotized, she cannot move her pale blue eyes and
she stumbles forward as water floods the sand and terror floods her brain.
Time feels like it slows as she goes
downward into the sea.
In the rainless storm, she knows she will be soaked;
the gulf engulfs her and she chokes.
She hears the scream of the deep… or is it her scream?
Simply put, she is trapped.
Trapped by unknown threats beneath the surface and the unforgiving riptide.
Trapped by whether or not she should sink or stay afloat.
Trapped,   trapped,   trapped…   until she is dead inside.

Angelina McGrath, PA, Avon Grove High School

Inhale and Exhale

"God. Why do you have to make everything so hard?"
His back falls in as he pushes himself out the door frame.
Hammered knees blushing with blue and black color the lifeless floor.
Magnified pieces of ceramic glass splinter the steak - it took all day to make
Inhale. Exhale. Collect yourself, woman.

Pointed toes balance her weight. She floats to the bathroom.
A fleshy heel touches the marble tile. Finally, some stability.
Sharp water from the shower camouflages horrific sounds of a weak girl.
"How could he say that?" A full turn of the handle. The water stops.
Swaddling the towel around. Eyes meet the mirror. A familiar countenance.

She recalls when she said "I'll break the cycle" "My life will be different"
She moisturized her hands after washing the dishes too "They'll stay soft."
Ignoring the knocking on the door. She rubbed lotion under her eyes.
It felt like sandpaper. Her skin; bright red. Fate was catching up.

"I'm sorry" and Inhale. Exhale. "It's been a long day" and Inhale. Exhale.
The door swings open. She stands with her shoulders tall. A slight tremor.
He hugs her. She looks past him. A frame of her mom. And daughter –
"It's fine," she says. Her nails dig into her palm. Bleeding crescents.

Her daughter asks at night; "Are you okay, Mommy?" Inhale and Exhale.
"I'm Perfect Junebug." And they both pretend it's true.
Kriti Saksena, NJ, Saddle River Day School

Pocket of Time

In a way, I have always been in love with summer
Thunderstorms, dark things
A promise of what I don't know
A secret a reformation a reverie
A trance
Like the world had held its breath all winter and the rush
of warm wind through the curtains
An exhale

Do you know what I mean when I say
I forget my own name
There is no talking allowed
Only roars, babbles, croaks,
sighs

I think I have always been in love with summer
Everything I do is an act of reaching for it, reaching towards
a scrap of silk slipping from my vision
Around some dark corner, a flash of a red hat, the familiar
blur of a jacket
Summer is a promise I never keep.
Arpita Acharya, IL, Plainfield North High School

The Smoke We Choose

My heart crumbles when I
Reflect that the coming generations
Will not know the sway of the trees
Nor the song of the breeze.

The scathing gaze of God pursues
As we suffocate ourselves
In the smoke that we choose
Over the gentle, hulking evergreen.

As time passes, the portrait of the American dream
Is morphing slowly from a luminescent green
To a somber gray—
To a concrete jungle scene.

This smog coats my lungs.
This dust chokes my throat.
And I cannot help but wonder
Can this beautiful world be saved?

For we've finally recognized the devastation
Our materialism has wrought.
But time may have left us behind
Because the final apocalypse has come from mankind.
Addy Thome, IL, University High School (Normal, IL)

stolen

what remains - what was

blurred laughter escapes steely confines - this bowl held ice cream
only do diamonds hide in haunting coal
through a glance, treasured memories whisper revenge upon theft
angry jewels urging mourners to craft blades in their searing heat
blind to this: will it be sweet?

hollow heart beats indifferent to time - home to glowing pulses
ask the sky for stars [to fade] then cower at sorrowful screeching
the tune of life must be lost to seek light in souls, warmth in bodies
hands reach up to beg, racing breaths deliver promises…regrets
children wish on the brightest stars: fuel towards destinies

rage sparked by a word, a step, a movement
a moment would ignite worse
light the flame
dance in it's heat
stare it to ashes
cry at its feet
smoke remains where she once was
swords can destroy homes
Sarah Malik, TX, Seven Lakes High School

Label-Libel

I've been thinking– a daughter, an Indian, a polyglot, a wild poet girl:
when someone asks to tell them about myself
I use these.
But what would introductions look like
if we said to each other, introduce without labels
GONE are our shorthands for understanding and seeing each other
gone the narrow distinctions of commonality and tribalism
what If I had to tell you everything
no nuance uncovered, no detail left behind

how I spent more days sobbing about the death of a book character
than the death of my grandmother
how there are piles of hair ripped out from frustration
that my Korean pronunciation doesn't sound quite right
how my family comes from a small rural town and now lives in the city
and holds the social benefits of none

what my great-great-great-great forefathers names are
what day and time my conception was (and all the other details, too)

why I wake up every morning and choose not to die

the full story of all the forces that converged to create the thing you see here
I imagine everyone would run out from the cocktail parties screaming.
Jyotika Aggarwal, NJ, West Windsor Plainsboro High School South

Desert

Allow me to lie in the midst of an ardent desert
My back against my old friend's warm body
My hair entombed in the sands who comprised you wholly
What else is there left that you don't embody?

Please, do not grant, a prudent creature to come near
With the company of two, we will never be so dear
Those who stand beyond the earth anathematize all day in their silly timbre
Their clicking leather boots drowning to less than rumble with no linger

My friend, it was just the two of us that day
Like a frivolous clown I danced on dreamily
While your sad, languid movements dragged on
Coaxing your frown I hummed your lullaby
Which I then whisper to you a song,
"Surely, a little dancing jaunt certainly requires no rush"
Then on and on under the moonlight we danced
With our drunken faces dawning, we blushed

With you, I am not afraid of flinty dirt scattered on my face
For once, with courtesy I will greet tomorrow's grace
Where, I am not afraid of shading to coffee tan
There, I will pretend I live a life so grand
Sherry Zhang, NJ, Ridgewood High School

Footprints of Hope

In fractured shoes, I tread memories,
Each step a trace of life's odyssey.
Through dusty paths, my village gleams,
A mosaic of poverty's silent screams.

India's embrace, fierce and cruel,
Violence etched in its sunburnt hue.
Broken streets, shattered dreams unfold,
A tapestry of stories left untold.

Yet, here in lands unknown, I stand,
A shadowed guest in this foreign land.
Whispers of hope weave my nights,
Stars above, my silent guides.

Golden fields replaced by city lights,
A stranger's heart in familiar sights.
Land of dreams, where hearts take flight,
Love and fear twine in silent fight.

I love this realm of boundless sky,
Though shadows linger, tears run dry.
For every step I take with grace,
In broken shoes, I find my place.

Nikhil Kashyap, WA, Henry M. Jackson High School

The Tsar's House

There's another party at the Tsar's house
This Tuesday at noon, and the revelry will peak
as the sun reaches its zenith in the sky.

When the tycoons pack the rooms
and when the palace can't fit another wasted king,
they say wine pours out of the windows
and it smells like France in the streets for weeks and weeks.
The washerwomen scrub the roads until their palms bleed,
but everyone knows why the bricks are red in the first place.

People say their grins are no canine and all fang,
the jackals in those rooms at the Tsar's house,
and they feed their wolves to their children
after throwing their pups to the dogs.
Not a single one exits the golden house without wine-stained teeth
and if you meet someone who swears his life on grape juice,
you'd best check his family portraits for his father's tinted smile.

The people on the ground are sick of wine, I hear
Patience and clothes wearing thinner each time they clean the Tsar's mess.
But others paint their teeth with pinot noir in the cloudy bathroom mirror,
and still others maintain that bricks are always that shade of maroon.

Lauren Wu, MA, Lexington High School

Growing Pains

Hometown, you are not
As sweet as I remember
Like burnt caramel
Coating the tongue
I listen to no birdsongs, no cricket choirs
The dragonflies have drowned in the paddies

I've lost you to the river
Downstream in the muck, the drain, sewage

The towers, edifices, rather, barricades
They pierce the fog, through to the sun
And the light bleeds down
Into the dirt

Spare change for the poor
Kicked aside by temple doors and
Melting like dark chocolate
In a child's clutch

I press my ear to the asphalt
Is it a heartbeat I hear?
It is the thunderous march
Of mercenaries, fallen in line

Athena Huynh, TX, John Paul II High School

Mother of Light

Mother, she held me within,
Surrounded in warmth in the dark.
I entered in horrible sin,
But her love lit me up like a spark.
    Oh, the glorious mothers of light!

When I'm scared and alone in the night,
She hears my loud call and is there.
My dear mother she cures me of fright,
She whispers a song through my hair.
    Oh, the wonderful mothers of light!

In the sunlight she flits between flowers,
I know her light step and her voice.
My mother grows bright in rain showers,
She loves all God's nature by choice.
    Oh, the beautiful mothers of light!

From her very first touch and her prayer,
To the dancing with stars overhead,
My mother has watched me with care,
And love from her red heart has bled.
    Oh, my beautiful mother of light.

Marin Evans, TX, Homeschool

The Mother: The Sea

Her voice, gentle and brutal, kind and harsh, pulls me from slumber
The moon is still up, the wide eye of heaven observing my every miniscule movement
As I return to *her*
I am nothing, but I believe I am everything when she engulfs me in loving, hateful arms
She is everything, the end and the beginning of life and death.
She has been here long before me, and she will be here long after.
I feel like an extension of her, as if I have returned to my roots the moment I set foot in
The Sea.
Her understanding, unforgiving waves pull me further out,
away from the land that binds me
I believe that I can hear her voice in her lapping, crashing waves
I do not know what she is saying, but I know it is something ancient and untranslatable
Something I could never understand, no matter how much I long to.
I wonder if Venus understood when she rose from the sea foam
She shares many traits with her mother: beauty and power, mercy and justice
The land is no longer visible, but I do not mind
The never-blinking eye of heaven still watches diligently, but I do not mind
How could I mind anything when I am home?
Abigail Duncan, TX, Frenship High School

    Pinpoint Stars

    To turn the point of a pin into a star
    Is the labor left by the fading light
    Creeping, clandestine, in folds along the horizon
    Trampled in haste at the silent birth of night

    Diligent, the dark races to its task
    To deliver in jest drowsy eyes and pillowed heads
    And to cloak with benevolent shadows all sharp things
    that cry unmasked

    With a child's wide eyes the night looks upon the unlookable
    And with a tear of mercy kisses its brow
    Draping in its sinking embrace all things that slice and scar
    Carving out only what is reverent, what is kind
    Carrying it bare and raw into Lily-white moonlight
    To the drowsy eyes pinched blind by the rosy hands of innocent night
    To all but the newly wrenched light of pinpoint stars
    Isabella Kapllani, NY, St. Anthony's High School

    When Mom Still Calls for Me

    The low haranguing of violet storm clouds
    Ushering me inside before I'm done kissing the flowers goodnight
    Bare feet are red and brown and in the shadowed light
    And they carry me—I corral all the crawling things
    Back into their homes, before the rain can have its way with them
    The door is open, and my mother is young,
    And I rumble back at the skies when she shuts the door behind me.
    Kieran Doyle, ID, Inspire Connections Academy

94 –My World

Behind Blue Eyes

I may be new here, but I know those eyes are not like the others.
    Wells of black ice under a starry night, accompanied by honey lips.
        Lost in the snow of her skin. Not bad for an outsider like me.

What's behind those blue eyes?
    They may seem like they're looking at you,
        but the truth is they are probably not, if they ever were.

They're nothing like me, but they're so predictable.
    Because, at night, when the moon rises, and its light shows her reflection,
        she is also lost in her gaze.

Although I know, that if I could, I would put them at their
    proper height, and I would show them things they have never seen.

But I also know that maybe I shouldn't look at them anymore,
    because in the depths of that sea of stars, lies the heart of darkness.
Jeronimo Munoz, MI, Walled Lake Western High School

    Clear Backpack

    I walked into school with a new backpack today
    Something stylish and hip and in with the times
    I got compliments on it from teachers and students alike

    But truthfully I don't really like it
    I wish I had my old backpack
    With the color and designs that were so much fun

    But I know that this is necessary
    I just wish it wasn't so
    I wish that school was normal again
    When we didn't have drills
    And we didn't have to wear these stupid backpacks

    I hate my clear backpack
    And I think I now hate school even more
    Riley Blondin, CO, River Ridge High School

        Forgotten Idols

        They are foreign to me now
        Three faces, similar and yet
        Worlds of difference

        Three sets of lifeless eyes
        Like the lifeless stars
        My body drifts upon

        Three puzzle pieces
        Seemingly correct and yet
        No matter how you configure them
        They just don't quite fit together.
    Katelyn Phillips, TX, Burleson Collegiate High School

Together we rise up

4 words said in the presence of justice being served
People of all backgrounds use their voices to be heard
TOGETHER a community can unite
Changing the way people go about life
4 words people march and chant for
When 1 voice brings so much more
WE as a nation still debate certain rights
To decide what is wrong and right we need to be precise
4 words used to make history
These words said clear cut delivery
RISE above social conformities
I've seen the people who protect also harm me as a minority
4 words this country used to weaponize
Although, only certain actions have been recognized
Any progress is good progress, as long as your going……..**UP.**
You either regret doing or not doing, and that's a fact.
Together we rise up
Andrea McElvaine, FL, Dr. Earl J. Lennard High School

The Peacock's Eyespot

The plume of feathery overture
Coated with the mirage of busy cities
They say it's for the best, it should be bright
The scintillating skyline sustained so that when
Dawn breaks and judgment arrives they can be fortunate
And so the forges churn incessantly, coughing up
Fracturing what little sky is left and any concert of repose
At inspection, it is a rattled snowglobe through gaunt glass
In a snowglobe factory through the perplexed fractals
On the shelves the fabric is drawn along with
A huddled disheveled crater in part of the gush brimming
As the snow and smog settles on a collage of 18 years past
The snowman stands in front of the skyscrapers, a feeble scarecrow
With voided eyes hollowed through the ashes of progress
Was I dragged down this pit by the spot?
Or by the fact everyone with me is still starstruck?
Aaryan Mishra, CA, Basis Independent Fremont Upper

Bujumbura

The sky is bright with rain falling out of it
The beautiful Tanganyika, right below it
The days go fast and are cold
The nature fills up, and around, and below
The city is cold and small
These locals quiet and calm
This place, is called... Bujumbura
Morenike Ayeni, CA, Fairmont Preparatory Academy

ElectroKiller

I must say,
my world has shrunk
shrunk from the wide-open blue skies, shrunk from the glistening stars
in the night sky,
shrunk from the far-out future, stretched along in front of me-
to the dull glow of a computer screen,
my eyes wavering, circled in bruised marks from too many late nights
wasted-
on this polychromatic glass box,
with its pleasures and tricks and surprises
all packaged into one,
one singular,
addicting monitor, the too-bright, jangling colors,
a reminder of how *bad* the world has made things-
things that were supposed to be good.
Lila Steele, AK, Alaska Middle College School

Boygirl Flame

June is ending,
soon fireworks will burst in the sky
an array of colors splitting like collapsing stars
and frightened dogs will scatter,
barking at the supernova

I dream of boyhood always, and it tastes like an epiphany
If heaven was in your sock drawer
And summer was never ending,
Sky pink by midnight and cicadas tucked into our ears
Sun an orange orb stuck beneath the pavement;
waiting to be caught
I could be such a pretty woman
but still I am chasing
Cameron Zhang, PA, Julia R. Masterman High School

Land of the Conquerors

You went red in the head   walked out into the dunes searching
for something with form   couldn't find it   only the sand's crest and
fall   the lost rhythm of life's heartbeat   the moon whiter than a rib
floating in the drifting bluets of the night   these lands are haunted
you know   these golden lands of promise   nothing ever happens and
nothing ever ends the angel says   and the barren thirst for it nearly
kills you   needless to say the mirage is always better   if faced with
the truth of things choose the empty air   you went red in the head
and this desert brute with history   brute with the silent masses swallowed
you whole   the heat tempers your molten glass red into the rib
white of the moon   suffering doesn't have to mean anything.
Surrender.
Audrey Aaltonen, CA, Huntington Beach High School

My World - 97

Perspective

I look out into the vast void of the world.
I see a bright light, surrounded by the darkness of night.
The light is pulsing far away
So hard to tell if it's charging through or staying at bay.
Hard to tell if it still stands a chance against the vast void
Or if the fight is already over, and the void has won
Slowly suffocating the light,
Till the job is done.
But I guess that what life is all about,
Perspective,
The way you look at something.
Cause you either see a shining light,
Bursting through the darkness.
Or a shining light, taking it's last couple of breaths,
Before being consumed,
By the vast void of the world.
Santyago Zapata, TX, Idea College Prep

The Ocean

Yesterday, a glittering blue.
Today, a murky grey-green.
The water changes colors like a mood ring, never predictable, never stable.

Yesterday, a disappointing ripple.
Today, a heaving, raging thing.
The waves roll upon themselves like a monster in its death throes,
thrashing in an agony of white spray and foam.

Yesterday, a soothing white noise,
Today, a dull, thundering boom
The sound is pleasant or frightening to the ear.

The ocean, loud and soft, gentle and strong, wild and calm, murky and clear.
Kayla Noelle Jennings , NC, Reformed Educational Institute

To Stand Divided

The deterioration of a nation is a symptom of a lack of transparency.
The government exists for the governed,
Yet, the treatment of citizens as expendable emerges as our downfall.

Like clockwork, a wave of hate will sweep over the land,
Bringing about a current of intolerance.
This intolerance captures our attention,
Emphasizing our differences.
It's common place for a battlefield of words to erupt,
Making our strength as a majority become fractured.

We are people with our vulnerabilities under fire,
Leading us to stand divided.
Shilo Lebowitz, NY, Oceanside High School

nighttime spirals

my head is swimming,
   my body leaden,
      my thoughts scattered

and dark,

as grim and pale

as the world outside

the rest of the house sleeps
while I break
   and crash
like silent waves
        on rocky shores, their noise stolen
by their solitude

"it'll be better in the morning,"
   I think blearily,

and I try to pretend

like it's the truth

Junwei Jonathan Tang, NY, Jericho Senior High School

The Wall

The wall wasn't always there.
Its construction was disguised.
No one saw it rising from the ground.
She didn't see it rising from the ground.

Her friends believed she had no wall.
They thought they knew her secrets.
They thought they knew her.
Shallow.
Gossip.
Annoying.
Roses bloomed to conceal it.
Yet, no one saw them rising from the ground.
She didn't see them rising from the ground.

Eventually, she recognized the wall.
She understood the wall.
For it had protected her,
It protected her family,
It protected her heart.
No one would see beyond that wall.
But, she could now see beyond that wall.

Caralina Lippincott, FL, Coral Reef Senior High School

My World

The Ocean

I often return to the ocean
The hot sands that tourists explore
I soak in the rays that burn some
I'm immune to the burn
A melanated superhero
Invincible
I let myself get pulled under the waves
If I stay there long enough I can hear them
My ancestor's voices
The voices of those who came by ship
Calling out to me
A myriad of encouragements mingle with the whale songs
You're stronger than you know
I feel safe here
Under the surface
Away from the hands of time
I'm with their
Fragments of bones that lie in this underwater land
The ones who understand
Ciera Roseboro, NC, Isaac Bear Early College

Running

An adrenaline-inducing escape from reality You,
Make the breath catch in my throat, make each breath
So valuable to take in You, are mind numbing and stress melting You,
Have a meter so easy to keep in pace with, every step I take in rhythm
To my heartbeat You, push every other thought away and keep the present from
Slipping away You, ground me, a cruel but sweet torture I cannot help
Indulge in, a kind gluttony in which I gladly partake

Medicine for the plagues of my mind, if not that, then a band aid
An insentient counsel, allowing me reprieve from the constant tumult of my
Thoughts I never thought, I could escape
I chase away the unseen afflictions clouding me,
Sometimes I manage to escape worry's grasp,
The blankness and quiet so comforting, so welcome
Umu Jalloh, GA, Gwinnett School of Mathematics, Science and Technology

Two-Year Flight

On return plane, the one of last year
By condition, through pupil, gazing close.
Wary, I flick the inner eye bigot seer
Preborn malignancies forced prostrate by pose.

Now wings stiff and engine then grumbling
And milky tea-leaves loosened of novelty new.
I'm looking for rhymes; wooled cortex tumbling —
Woolly it may be but nether-troubles in queue.
Jamie Haenisch, CA, Polytechnic School

100 –My World

A War Against the Soul (Modern Days)

Trapped at home, the sheer bleakness of life is apparent.
Without the murmuring world, the company of even the city rats seems overwhelming.
As emptiness envelops the cities through cracked-out radio, destruction is imminent.
Bring down the mundane plaster of my living room,
and allow me to dance on the blue-black streets once more.

A dancer spins freest in the torrent of sound, picked up on symphony swells of tide.
Over the seaweed castles and kelp towers of the locker-bound.
Under the shadows of the few travelers still wandering the desolate seas.
Open arms swallowed, torn asunder by the galloping hoof-beats of white-capped horses,
you swirl faster than a tornado, hungry for motion, with the gorging grace of a hurricane.

You fight a vision, in the lace-black of a funeral queen, dolled up for hell's afterparty.
A ghost of 1920, she's unnaturally alive- a killer who cannot be killed.
Her crown of poison-green, cherry-red, and oceanic blue is imprinted upon your mind.
Dripping scarlet oil-spots over velvet, oozing slack-jawed from knifed canines,
she smiled, turning body against itself, trapping mind in a keyless prison.

Manically, musically, you pirouette through the empty streets, the moon on your back.
Before you fall into fitful slumber, you sing out of your floral-swathed window.
The morning birds, fed on apartment trash, catch your drift and harmonize.
I wait for the sky-slicing gilt of the fall sunrise over the cosmopolitan malls,
showering stores we'd frequent in 2016, before life became a war between mind and soul.
Danica McCarron, NC, Cary Academy

Ana Jane

Oh the pathological honesty
Of the young girl Ana Jane
She will tell the truth constantly
but the lies of others will be her bane

She craves authenticity
She never wants to deceive
Her wagers are always fair
To her opponents she is naive

You can see it in her face,
When someone who doesn't play by the rules
Wins the race

It breaks her inside to know that cheaters can gain
And all the work that she has done
Has simply been in vain

She's never told a lie
And she's never
Won the chase
Held back by her morals
Ana Jane: a true disgrace

Cecilia Caroline Barrios, LA, Saint Louis Catholic High School

My World - 101

The Nature of Abandon

Abandonment is a natural thing
The fear of it even more natural
Chicks in their nests must fear being abandoned by their mothers
Creatures in tide pools must fear being abandoned by the sea
Often you are not abandoned by entities you want but those you feel you need

The yin to your yang never really feels like its there
Until it's not
The moon doesn't miss the sun
Until the sun no longer makes the moon shine
The stars must simply watch as bystanders to a scar
that will mar their divine surfaces for centuries

It feels impossible to survive once abandoned
Unfinished sculptures without their creators
will forever reach for their unattainable potential
Without it's master a home will decay until it's nothing more than a couple of bricks
and a whisper of the life that once entwined itself with every atom of the place

Hopelessness is natural, but hope is just as constant
The romantics will see a creature desecrated and torn and see it for its beauty
Because for every chick without a mother there is a mother without a chick
For every lost soul there is another in the same maze of despair that seeks solace
Change is natural, Abandonment is never permanent
Olivia Barlitt, CO, Rampart High School

                Simply Won't Grow

                On December the twenty-first
                I decided my tree to nurse.
                Because my little Christmas tree
                measured a measly four foot three.
                Proper ones are eight feet you know
                to reach that great height it must grow.
                I remembered a fact from school
                that trees use water as a fuel.
                So into the bath, I threw it
                I turned on the tap, thought a bit
                then added a dash of shampoo.
                After all what harm could it do?
                Just as I could taste triumph sweet
                I heard at once the sound of feet.
                The bathroom door it opened wide
                "What are you doing!" mother cried.
                "Making my small tree grow," I said.
                She laughed, "How empty is your head?
                My dear child how can you not know
                plastic trees simply do not grow."
                John Dean, TX, Homeschooled

to disappear

my grandmother has worn the same perfume all her life; she envelops her skin in apricots
languished by the summer sun until wrinkled, like her fingers when i help her from the
tub, careful not to let her slip; one slip & she might just shatter—memories locked in
a fragile colosseum of bone so i lay the bedsheet on her body as one touches the
untouchable—*stroke a butterfly's wings and you'll see what i mean*
crawl into her brain and watch the ashes of anamnesis spill
out onto the bathroom floor, try to pick them up but
they'll keep falling through the gaps of your
virgin hands, watch her dissipate
till she is nothing but dust,
and apricots in the
air.
Soleil Ava Wizman, NY, Hunter College High School

    Mudpies, Jump Roping, Fairy Dust, and Cartwheels

    The little girl tugs at my hands
    Her palms are sweaty from jump roping
    There is dirt underneath her fingernails from baking mud pies
    Her ebony hair is knotted and messy from doing cartwheels beneath the sun
    We are alone, the little girl and I
    We eat ice cream and wear dandelion crowns
    Under the hot sun, the ice cream turns into
    A colorful, sugary slush
    Dripping down our chins, onto our sweaty palms, between our dirty fingernails
    Settling upon our ebony hair like fairy dust
    Strawberry slush streams through our veins,
    Cotton candy pours out of our noses,
    Fat diamond beads of pistachio race down our eyes
    A salty, sugary mixture pools at our feet
    We have *everything* and we have *nothing*
    But *nothing* is perfectly enough
    for the little girl and I
    Clare Wong, CA, Sage Creek High School

From What Do You Come?

"where do you come from?"
    america.
"where are you actually from?"
    california…
"no, like where are you from?"
    from a pear: the Womb of my Mother.
"no, like actually?"
    from the Laughter of the Waves & Wind/from the Love of the Sun & the Moon
"no, where."
    what more is there to come from than the Bees, Soil, Milk, and Light?
"you don't understa-"
    do You?
Michelle Chen, CA, 95128— Saint Francis High School Mountain View

My World - 103

Where I am From

There used to be small wooden houses with straw roof tops here
People clad in silk garments and bamboo framed hats walked the dirt streets here
Everyone was bound by the unquestioned hierarchy here
But still collectively guided by the principles of Confucius.

One day men in oversized suits and american accents came here
They changed the ideological scene here
They replaced the King for a president here
Factories and industry became the new thing here

Now there is not a street without bustling traffic here
A block without a frontier of steel buildings that line the sky here
The night never seems to be quiet here
Traditional architecture and norms are now hard to find here.

A new era has emerged here.
But it is still the city that I learned to ride a bike in
It is still the city that my parents grew up in.
It is still the city that I call home.

I am from Seoul, South Korea.

Justin Kang, NJ, The Taft School

          Fossils

          Surreptitiously, we own our colors,
          every day, the grays and the reds,
          the massively swollen purple fractures
          of half-truths and white lies.
          No one leaves without lessons,
          the fault line of life,   severed,
          cracked, broken,   eroded,
          never again matching, puzzle
          pieces, missing and worn.

          What is, what was,
          what would have, could have,
          should have been,
          squatters in the shale,
          cliff to cliff, edge to edge,
          evidence of a life lived,
          beaten d   r come,
                o   e
              w   v
           n but o
          fossilized forever
       through faith & perseverance.
       Dwight E. Dieter, NJ, editor

Table of Authors

Aaltonen, Audrey - 97	Land of the Conquerors
Acharya, Arpita - 89	Pocket of Time
Adams, Camryn - 34	The Lonely Bones Poem
Aggarwal, Jyotika - 91	Label-Libel
Aguila-Velez, Preston - 25	Eternal Loves Journey
Ahn, Hannah - 34	This Is What We Talk About...
Akhmedova, Diana - 20	Sleepless Nights Thinking About You
Aman, Meron - 80	I, too
Amiri, Liv - 86	11 AM Matinee
Andersen, Ellie - 15	The Storm
Anireddy, Hasini - 37	A Letter from a Belt...
Arrington, Aiden - 33	A2 Masterpiece
Ashford, Iliana - 4	Murrah Building Bombing
Ayeni, Morenike - 96	Bujumbura
Babalola, Ileri - 87	Dammed River
Bah, Binta - 63	Offers Made to Prosper
Bailey, Meigan - 43	Failure My Dear
Balasubramanya, Ananya - 57	Icarus Unburned
Bandy, Valens - 32	Simple Devotion
Baqai, Anousha - 78	A Narcissist's Failure
Barenholtz, Tova - 9	Unveiling Society's Mask
Barlitt, Olivia - 102	The Nature of Abandon
Barrios, Cecilia Caroline - 101	Ana Jane
Barton, Alexis - 40	Cut the Grass
Bates, Ryan - 56	Why am I about to drown?
Benton, Miles - 38	a casket of gold
Berzoza, Lily - 71	I am
Blondin, Riley - 95	Clear Backpack
Boyer, Lillian - 47	Petals of Violet
Bradley, Briseis - 76	Behind Locked Doors
Branflick, Haley - 54	A Force of Nature
Brodsky, Nikole - 84	A Faint Summer Morning
Bui, Tuyet Kha - 50	Bye or Thank you?
Bullinger, Nate - 30	To Nonno, A Promise
Bunao, Ava - 41	when caterpillars become men
Burns, Sean - 88	Rivers of Ink
Calkin, Caleb - 55	Bonfire
Cammack, Samantha - 16	Past, Present, and Future
Carandang, Angela - 31	Garden of Sapphire
Carpenter, Majesty - 51	Roses
Carter, Charisma - 3	A Heart's Thoughts
Cash, Sevan - 81	Սխսթյուն
Chao, Emily - 7	The Means to Pray

Charbonneau, Chloe - 36	Hunger
Chen, Jeffrey - 26	Silent Flames, Love in Shadows
Chen, Michelle - 103	From What Do You Come?
Chen, Rexana - 79	A Vast Sea of Possibility
Cho, Hongju - 79	Acculturation
Clark, Samantha - 65	Camouflage Bijou
Collins, Lily - 69	A Smiling Stranger
Confer, Eli - 69	Entry Denied
Connell, Lainey Nicole - 64	Maladaptive Daydreams
Cornett, Elizabeth - 35	An Orange for our woes
Cross, John - 61	Raindrops for the Soul
Cruz, Jhaylin - 12	The Struggle for Survival
Dean, John - 102	Simply Won't Grow
Demming, J'Auna - 44	Like My Mother, I Am an Enigma
Desmarais, Hailey - 13	Grandmother
Diallo, Fatima - 13	To Be Free
Dieter, Dwight E. - 104	Fossils
Dieter, Dwight E. - 18	Beating Back the Forest
Do, Quan - 85	Eternal Embrace
Doran, Danielle - 21	drizzle
Doyle, Kieran - 94	When Mom Still Calls for Me
Driessen, Daniel - 60	The Dream is Questioned
Duncan, Abigail - 94	The Mother: The Sea
English, Adyanna - 32	L. O. V. E.
Esan, Ikeoluwa - 46	Right Now
Evans, Marin - 93	Mother of Light
Farooqui, Hanaa - 74	the silence is deafening
Fuentes, Thalia - 28	Oh Mother, How Mother
Garnica, Abigail - 75	Circling Back
Gibson, Declan Quinn - 26	Dear Rosebud
Gibson, Erika - 33	When the Film Develops
Graham, Reagan - 72	Dyslexia
Guerra, Gabriella - 29	Between Held Hands
Haddad, Yasmina - 82	On hearing the bus park at my stop
Haenisch, Jamie - 100	Two-Year Flight
Hamed, Taleen - 15	Whispers of the Night
Hankins, Tucker - 58	Invincible
Heng, Victoria - 70	i have known the moon
Henry, Elise - 56	Leak
Hernandez, Adanahi - 24	To Jirón
Hernandez, Lucy - 23	Whispers of the Aching Heart
Hill, Avi - 2	The Light
Hilliker, Leilah - 4	Healing the Scars of Asian Hate
Hoeper, Victoria - 22	Admiration
Holandez, Angelina - 58	Seasonal Depression
Huynh, Athena - 93	Growing Pains
Ilas, Kaya - 48	Her laughs
Jalloh, Umu - 100	Running
Jenkinson, Maria - 57	The Eye of the Storm
Jantzen, Ayden – 59	snowman story

Jennings, Kayla Noelle - 98	The Ocean
Job, Stephanie - 80	Grieving Red Hand
Jones, Gates Lilybet - 41	Driving is all the weight...
Kang, Alysa - 47	Waves, Snakes & Hawks
Kang, Justin - 104	Where I am From
Kapllani, Isabella - 94	Pinpoint Stars
Kapllani, Rachel - 45	A Precious Heirloom
Kashyap, Nikhil - 92	Footprints of Hope
Kaur, Sharndeep - 8	Butterfly Insanity
Khanom, Mosammad - 82	Staring Contest
Kibet, Brevia - 70	The pressure of being
Kim, Angie Minjung - 81	The Whale
Kini, Nina - 51	Ink Parlour
Klusek, Azure - 20	Protagonists
Krugh, Katherine - 65	To Be Just Me, Again
Kuate, Legend - 25	Waves
Larson, Katherine - 68	Cheater
Lawing, Casey - 36	El Podor del Languaje
Layton, Emersyn - 65	The house in Which I was raised
Lebowitz, Shilo - 98	To Stand Divided
Lippincott, Caralina - 99	The Wall
Lovell, Charlotte - 30	Magical Moonlit Waltz
Mailhot, Mindy - 10	Dear Universe
Malcuit, Audrey - 63	Purgatory
Malik, Sarah - 90	stolen
Manahan, Derek - 53	Bittersweet Lies
Manning, Morgan P. - 49	The Influence of Aphrodite
Margheim, Avienda - 42	Time Dreams
Marin, Emily - 17	A Tribute to All
Markey, Natalya - 49	The Sight
Martinez, Araylia-marie - 84	Where I'm From
Martinez, Gavin - 71	Collide
Mason, Azara - 61	Fight, Flight, Freeze in Giovanni's Room
McCarron, Danica - 101	A War Against the Soul
McElvaine, Andrea - 96	Together we rise up
McGiffin, Michael - 11	Heaven's Gate
McGrath, Angelina - 88	Trapped
McKinney, Kendall - 64	overwhelming in great awe
McNeal, Brazil - 73	Nothing But
Meikle, Jessica - 14	Celestial Adventure
Melton, Emma - 11	How We Are Forced to Think
Mike, Evangelia - 62	Words of the Winded
Mishra, Aaryan - 96	The Peacock's Eyespot
Mohan, Ria - 27	Pinky Promise
Molinero-Montiel, Jamile - 63	The Disappearance of Me
Moore, Autumn - 35	Coconut
Moye, Judah - 11	The Potter
Muirhead, Alexa - 5	The Question of What
Munoz, Jeronimo - 95	Behind Blue Eyes
Nasir, Adelia – 29	The Color Blue

Newby, Lillian - 46	You Know
Nguyen, Huyen Amy Van - 52	A Greedy Craving for the Void
Nguyen, Kellye - 22	Painting
Obiakonwa, Onyinyechi - 64	A diary's burden
Oduntan, Oluseyi - 67	The Summer Before Senior Year
Pahuja, Mehul - 85	Always?
Pak, Lyla - 21	Words left unsaid
Palik, Joshua - 14	Plans
Phillips, Katelyn - 95	Forgotten Idols
Phillips, Maggie - 13	Rosa
Pilla, Karishma - 83	stripped
Principe, Clara - 52	Half a Conversation
Ramos, Yadira - 9	The Greatest Mystery
Reyes, Jocelyn Valentin - 75	The Grand Stairwell
Richardson, Asha - 18	Play
Robertson, Katelynn - 50	Thread
Robinson, Natalie - 59	Air, The Unseen Soul Remedy
Roseboro, Ciera - 100	The Ocean
Roundtree, Tiana - 15	Flawless Shape
Rubel, Brendan - 6	Today
Saksena, Kriti - 89	Inhale and Exhale
Samano, Brianna Chanel - 66	What Can an Angry Woman Do?
Sanders, Isaac - 7	Seeds for a Time without Flowers
Schlesinger, Julia - 42	She Knows the Future
Schmidt, Jane A. - 12	Ode to the Thieving Gardener
Scurek, Addison - 37	The Price of Love
Seyal, Rayaan - 53	Whispers Within A Solitary Mind's…
Shah, Foram - 43	deconstructed sonnet to misogyny
Sharma, Riddhi - 86	Hush...
Sherwin, Corinne - 78	What Happens
Shook, Cailee Grace - 38	where water meets land
Simpson, Max-Ryker Sparks - 72	Lord of Larvae
Sizemore, Haley (Shiloh) - 27	Saffron
Smith, Gabriella - 33	Break you beautifully
Smith, Sienna - 72	Santa Barbara
Soldevilla, Annabella Rose - 74	Awake
Sommerhauser, Amelia - 67	When Cold Hands Touch
Speller, Sydney - 66	Winding World
Spiewak, Karolina - 60	Cobs & Pens
Sproul, Kacie - 24	Seven Hundred and Thirty Days
Staed, Jacob - 31	That of Icarus
Steele, Lila - 97	ElectroKiller
Taffere, Millena - 12	Reign of Sun
Tang, Junwei Jonathan - 99	nighttime spirals
Taylor, Julianna - 6	Midnight
Thaman, Nikolai - 8	She was
Thao, Pahlychai - 62	Ghosts
Thome, Addy - 90	The Smoke We Choose
Thompson, Ava - 35	He Notices
Tian, Alice – 40	to leave a loveless link

Tran, Jennifer - 83	Nail Bar
Tran, Thuy-An Elizabeth - 48	Birthday Candle
Turcotte, Lily - 32	all or none
Vaughn, Jack - 44	new beginning
Vecchioni, Jeremiah - 66	Those Dreams on the Shelf
Vu, Emily - 16	Life in Seasons
Vuppala, Ananya - 87	Lights
Walker, Marisol - 10	Searching
Wallwork, Gryffin Daniel - 3	Wonders of the Seasons
Walter, Emma - 74	NUMB
Ward, Laila - 62	Beauty Standards
Warnsley, Dakota - 68	Two sides of the same coin
Webster, Titus - 2	To Death
Weicht, Reese - 17	Prince of Peace
White, Jayden - 31	My Own
Wiechman, Carys - 55	She had words on the tip of her tongue...
Willett, Alyssa - 5	Before the Dawn
Williams, Jadzia - 14	Nature
Wilson, Izabel - 70	The Chapel Window
Wizman, Soleil Ava - 103	to disappear
Wolfs, Brooklyn - 73	My Anxiety
Wong, Clare - 103	Mudpies, Jump Roping, Fairy Dust...
Woyte, Mackenzie Noelle - 54	Waterfall Feelings
Wright, Eva - 68	Grief
Wu, Lauren - 92	The Tsar's House
Wytaske, Carly - 45	Racing Thoughts
Yango, Lyla - 28	this is how it began...
Yih, Charlotte - 67	lineage
Yos, Melissa - 23	Letter to A. Gong
Zapata, Santyago - 98	Perspective
Zhang, Cameron - 97	Boygirl Flame
Zhang, Sherry - 91	Desert

***

Our topical anthologies have been providing opportunities for
for young poets to share their poetry with other likeminded individuals
since 1998.

We have survived these twenty-five years because of our commitment
to selecting only those poems which we feel have meaning
and the ability to speak to our readers where they are.

We thank all of you who have participated
and have helped us achieve that vision

***

other Live Poets Society of NJ books available on Amazon

Fossils
by Dwight Edward Dieter
our founder and editor
ISBN: 9798365661356

"…evidence of a life lived, beaten down, but overcome,
fossilized forever, through faith and perseverance."

This collection contains Mr. Dieter's first seven chapbooks,
and shows, not only the natural progression in his writing,
but also the natural progression of a life well-lived,
full of questions, searching, and irony, It is recommended
for all young writers who feel anxious about the future,
weighed down by the present, and saddled with the past.

Made in the USA
Coppell, TX
25 September 2023